Explore the Possibilities

Ultimately we can never know for sure whether channeling is a fabrication of our own minds, or true communication with other beings. But the way I look at it, if we have invented all these channelings, the human mind has an amazing capacity to access wisdom far beyond our conscious knowledge. And if we have not made it up, then the universe is full of many wise beings who love us and want to help us.

Pick your miracle . . .

ABOUT THE AUTHOR

KATHRYN RIDALL, Ph.D., holds advanced degrees from the California School of Professional Psychology and from the California Institute of Integral Studies. For more than a decade, she worked as a counselor, social worker, administrator in traditional mental health facilities specializing in child abuse prevention and the treatment of severely disturbed children. For the past seven years she has worked as a psychic counselor, integrating spiritual disciplines with psychotherapeutic techniques. She currently has practices in both Northern and Southern California where she teaches workshops on intuitive development as well as offering private psychic consultations.

CHANNELING
How to Reach Out
to
Your Spirit Guides

Kathryn Ridall, Ph.D.

Produced by The Philip Lief Group, Inc.

BANTAM BOOKS
TORONTO · NEW YORK · LONDON · SYDNEY · AUCKLAND

This book is dedicated to Tobi Sanders, who helped to give New Age thought a voice and to my many spirit friends who have loved me well.

CHANNELING

A Bantam Book / March 1988

ISBN 0-553-27181-4

Published simultaneously in the United States and Canada

Bantam Books are published by Bantam Books, a division of Bantam Doubleday Dell Publishing Group, Inc. Its trademark, consisting of the words "Bantam Books" and the portrayal of a rooster, is Registered in U.S. Patent and Trademark Office and in other countries. Marca Registrada. Bantam Books, 666 Fifth Avenue, New York, New York 10103.

PRINTED IN THE UNITED STATES OF AMERICA

O   0 9 8 7 6 5 4 3 2 1

Acknowledgments

To Scott Catamas, my friend and partner, whose love and support makes all things possible.

To Jerie Gilbert, who connected me with this book and so much more. To Jackie Dennis and Joanna Bongiovanni, with whom I have explored intuitive worlds. To Richard Ryal, who introduced me to channeling.

To the many friends of this book, especially: Sanaya Roman, Thom Elkjer, Darryl Anka, Professor Jonathan Klimo, Dr. Margo Chandley, Carole Hoss, Judith Cornell, Susan Levin, Rebekah Conner, Michael Reed Gach, and Sherri Kahn.

To Kevin Osborn, the most sensitive, astute editor I could have asked for. To Brad Bunnin, for a speedy legal education. To Barbara Alpert and the staff at Bantam for stepping in and picking up this project with so much enthusiasm. To Philip Lief, who put this all together with clarity and fairness.

Finally, and not least important, I want to acknowledge my indebtedness to Edgar Cayce and Jane Roberts and the other pioneers in channeling, whose courage made my book so easy to write.

Contents

Introduction

For the past five years I have been involved in a wonderful adventure in consciousness called channeling. Channeling is the ability to connect with other beings and other levels of consciousness and to express their reality through our body. A channel acts as an intermediary between our physical world and the unseen dimensions of the universe. You could think of a channel as a living transmitter of subtle energies, much like a telephone or a radio station.

This description might sound esoteric, but in fact channeling is a very natural and easy process. We all have the ability to open ourselves to other realms of consciousness and to use that contact to enrich and enlighten our lives.

During the five years that I have been involved in channeling, my understanding of consciousness, of the nature of the universe, and of my own inner being have shifted dramatically. I would like to share some of my own experiences of channeling with you. Hopefully my experiences and the experiences of others included in this book will inspire you to embark on this adventure yourself.

Meeting Diya

My first introduction to channeling came while I was living in the San Francisco Bay Area in 1983. A respected friend had invited me to her home to hear Richard Ryal, a local channel. At the time I was writing my doctoral dissertation and had advanced along a path of psychological and spiritual growth for fifteen years. I had studied Western psychologies and Eastern philosophy and meditation. I had also worked as a social worker and counselor for many years.

When I first received this invitation, I had mixed feelings about going to hear a channel. Although I had spent years exploring consciousness, my only previous contact with channeling had come through the books of Edgar Cayce and Jane Roberts, writings which had deeply affected me. In fact, I had derived two of my basic beliefs about the world—that we create every aspect of our own reality and that we are multidimensional beings who simultaneously experience many dimensions of reality—from reading the Seth material by Roberts. My contact with these books had played a crucial role in developing my spiritual consciousness. In retrospect, I would say that my reading of the Seth books had made me receptive to the idea that I might benefit from teachers on other levels of existence and that channeled information could be valuable to me. And, although I was not aware of this at the time, reading the Seth books had whetted my appetite for learning how to access this kind of material myself.

On the other hand, although Jane Roberts had meant so much to me, I actually had many prejudices against channeling. I had never seen a trance channel: The proliferation of channels that we saw in the mid-eighties had not occurred, and channeling had not yet become a popular part of New Age or metaphysical experience. My friends and clients had not yet begun to tell me of their extraordinary encounters with channels. And after years of watching horror movies, I had retained residual fears of being taken over by malevolent spirits. Most importantly, my years of studying Eastern philosophy had left me with the idea that working with spirit guides could only distract me from experiencing my own deepest nature. If someone had asked me how I pictured a typical channel, I would have joked about little old ladies with Ouija boards and neurotic cats, or greedy charlatans who exploited the little old ladies with the neurotic cats.

Given these prejudices, I was much surprised when I met Richard. An attractive, intelligent man, Richard quickly went into trance and brought forth a being called Diya. I witnessed neither epileptic seizures nor dramatic changes of personality. Richard's voice merely deepened and took on an added resonance.

Diya gave me a strong first impression that I was indeed in the presence of a powerful being. His message about the importance of attuning to other beings and to the earth itself as a basis for creating joy and harmony in life resonated deeply within me. I also welcomed his offer to "amplify and clarify" the energy in different centers of the body so that we could attune more fully to each other and the earth. The fact that I could feel subtle energies moving in my heart and in my brain stem during this powerful activation of energy helped me to believe that something real was happening.

After that initial evening, I went to several more meetings; Diya impressed me more and more with each new experience. I eventually signed up for a year-long healer's training that Richard and Diya had offered to teach. During the year that I attended these training sessions, I grew to know both Richard and Diya and was able to distinguish between their personalities and perspectives. I also grew to love Diya as a teacher and friend. I learned to trust his personal guidance and to cherish his wisdom and compassion.

One of the most powerful proofs to me that something powerful was happening was my tendency to go unconscious ten minutes after Diya began his lecture. Every week I would resolve to remain fully conscious, but every week I would inevitably lose consciousness. Yet I did not find this experience frightening. Partially, I remained calm about this loss of consciousness because I was with friends whom I trusted. However, I also returned from these unconscious spells feeling revitalized, refreshed, and with the sense that I had had an important experience. As I now understand this phenomenon, I was unable to attune consciously to Diya and communicate with him due to the limitations of my own personality. So I would leave my body to allow a fuller contact to occur. I believe that these out-of-body experiences prepared me for conscious channeling.

Beginning to Channel

Almost exactly a year after I met Diya, I began to experience a slight pressure on the left side of my head. I could feel a stream of words, a channel of communication available for me to tune in to if I so decided. By this time I had so much love and respect for Diya that my initial fears that he might overwhelm me or distract me from my own inner nature had all but disappeared. I easily made the decision to try to channel.

I first learned to channel by turning on a tape recorder and allowing the stream of words in my left brain to come through my mouth. My first channeling experience lasted only twenty minutes, but I felt exhausted afterward. My body did not yet have the stamina to merge with another being without feeling some stress.

I reacted to my first channeling experience with mixed emotions. On the most fundamental level it felt natural. Because I had worked with Diya for a year, I had already learned to trust him and to feel a deep love for him. That year had served as a bridge, allowing me to feel that channeling him myself would provide a natural extension of the intimacy I had felt toward him for a long time.

I also felt excited, because I knew that I was opening myself up to an entirely new level of experience. I felt a bit like a pioneer heading out into the inner frontiers. I also felt some pride and exhilaration. Even after watching Richard Ryal channel Diya for a year, I did not feel confident in my own ability to channel. In fact, I seriously doubted whether I could channel, so I was delighted to discover this new capacity in myself.

Finally, although the process of channeling felt natural and my connection to Diya felt safe and comfortable, I felt surprised at the actual content of the material I channeled. Diya's first words to me were, "We would like to assure you that angels do indeed exist." Since angels were definitely not part of the world view of my twentieth-century mind, this statement surprised and even unsettled me. This surprise at thoughts so different from my own, because it confirmed that I was experiencing something other than my normal perception, strongly influenced my belief in channeling as a phenomenon outside of myself.

Aside from my astonishment, my most pronounced experience was energetic. Usually I feel as if my awareness and attention wander in many different directions simultaneously, but when I channeled, I felt very contained energetically. I felt as though I had drawn all of my energy into the central core of my body and that a stream of deeply vibrating energy had rooted me to the earth. I found this feeling of deep focus extremely nourishing, as if I were being fed on some subtle energetic level.

Putting Skepticism Aside

After my first channeling experience, I practiced every day. Because I liked that subtle sense of energetic nourishment, and the novelty of Diya's ideas fascinated and intrigued me, I wanted to channel as much as possible. Diya's early teachings focused on expanding my views of conscious life in the universe. He taught me that the human evolutionary chain represents just one of millions of evolutionary chains. He taught me not only that many planets and solar systems support life, but that many dimensions of nonphysical consciousness exist as well. He taught me that the universe literally teems with life and that we have the ability to attune to and establish telepathic rapport with many beings.

My early obsession with daily channeling also grew out of my skepticism. I wanted to know if this channel-

ing was "real," and so spent hours listening to the
tapes, analyzing them for their form and content. I
wanted to see if I could truly distinguish between
Diya's ideas and mine, between Diya's style of presen-
tation and mine. Although I had been a spiritual seeker
for years, part of me still only believed in the evidence
of the five senses, and I wanted to make sure that this
channeling was more than my imagination.

When I listened to the tapes, I noticed several
differences. For one thing, when I channeled, I didn't
use the same speech patterns I normally used. I seemed
to breathe more shallowly and less often, my pitch was
lower, and I intoned words differently. Although I
might have regarded these distinctions as a by-product
of trance rather than as definitive proof of the existence
of an independent being, they did show me that I had
at the very least entered another state of consciousness.

I also noticed a difference in language patterns and
syntax. I tend to speak and write in short, somewhat
clipped sentences. But the material I received from
Diya came in long sentences with extended metaphors.
Where I tend to understate, Diya tended to pontificate.
I punctuate my sentences with mannerisms such as
"you know." The channeled information, however, never included any of these language fillers that I have
come to depend on. I talk in short paragraphs and do
not tend to tell stories or speak in monologues, but
Diya talked for forty-five minutes, relating perfectly
crafted ideas and systematically building from one idea
to another.

Finally, the content of the channeled material
contrasted sharply with that of my conscious personality. A fairly provincial earthling, I had given little thought
to angels or other paths of evolution.

Through watching myself as I channeled and listening to the tapes afterward, I saw many differences
between Diya's style and perspectives and my own.
However, I eventually decided that I would probably
never know for sure whether Diya was simply an
aspect of my own consciousness or an independent
being. And I ultimately concluded that it didn't matter

where the information came from as long as the experience was valuable for me. I realized that it didn't matter if it was "just" my imagination, for even that explanation would mean that my mind was a far richer and far more complex instrument than I had previously imagined. I resolved to stop trying to decide the undecidable and to explore where channeling could take me and how it could raise my consciousness, rather than worrying about whether it was real or not.

Early Gifts from Diya

In addition to the broadened perspective I mentioned earlier, I received many gifts from Diya during those early days of channeling. His teachings about the nature of the universe expanded my views of conscious life, relieving me of the twentieth-century belief that human existence is merely a kind of genetic aberration in an uncaring universe.

He also taught me about love. His teachings were simple. Love is the glue of the universe, the force of attraction which binds together molecules and holds together all form. Although very simple, these teachings—when properly understood—were very radical. However, Diya's teaching about love came much more through my experience of him than through his words. I felt deeply and completely loved by him. I found it very healing to be loved by someone who saw all my strengths and weaknesses. The knowledge that love for the human race exists throughout the universe was equally healing.

Diya also gave me a final gift, one more psychological in nature. As soon as I began to channel, Diya started to provide personal information and guidance. He helped me understand my personal motivations in a different way and offered brilliant, if sometimes unflattering, analyses of my personality. He knew exactly what my weaknesses were and pushed me to correct them. One of his most important psychological messages to me was to avoid giving personal authority or responsibility over to any teacher, whether that teacher came to me as a priest, guru, or spirit guide. Like most good teachers, Diya taught that the function of any true teacher is to help us see the God in ourselves, to know our own multidimensional beings. The teacher's job is to reflect our own inner nature to us and to help us reach our own unique expression of that inner nature. Too often, however, we tend to emulate our teachers' paths rather than finding our own way to the state of consciousness we see in them. Too often we become like children seeking the answers from an all-knowing mother or father.

Diya pointed out my own tendency to concede authority every time it appeared, whether it arose in relationship to himself or to others, and he showed me how that tendency undermined my own sense of personal power. Early on he told me that I had chosen a discarnate teacher because I knew unconsciously that it would be difficult to emulate or imitate a being that didn't have a body. Working with a discarnate teacher decreased the temptation to pattern my life after his, forcing me to move toward my own truth and my own creative self-expression.

Teaching Others to Channel

A few months after I began to channel Diya, my friends and psychotherapy clients began to ask me to teach them to channel. At first I felt reluctant. Since no one had really taught me to channel, I did not have a technique to offer. When I turned to Diya for help, he immediately presented me with the technique detailed in this book.

My experience in teaching others has offered me confirmation of Diya's teaching that the universe is full of many life forms. All individuals draw to themselves a teaching entity well-suited to their particular strengths and weaknesses, skills and temperament. Whether one chooses to tune in consciously to those guides or not, they are there. As I have helped other people connect consciously with their guides and draw new guides to them, I have gotten to know a wide assortment of guides. I have had the opportunity to meet a Taoist yogi, a Native American shaman, angelic beings, beings from other planets, and nature sprites.

Perhaps the most interesting guides I've encountered called themselves the Committee. The Committee was comprised of a line, a spiral, and a multidimensional triangle. The woman who channeled them, although thoroughly trained in art history and the healing arts, had to begin to study physics in order to communicate with them. Their intelligence and consciousness was very foreign to the channel, and yet when she first began to channel them, she felt a love between herself and these geometric consciousnesses that brought tears to her eyes.

When I tell this story, people often wonder how she could have channeled a geometric intelligence. Although she might have connected with a very different kind of life form, which *she* likened to or translated as geometric forms, I find it plausible to think of it in terms of energy flow. Every form has an intelligence or energy behind it, a concept or a metaphysical idea behind its concrete form. Every geometric form has a certain flow of energy connected with it. For instance, the line as she channeled it was vertical. The Committee explained to her that the line represented the movement from abstract thought to matter, from spirit to form, and that the line was here to teach her about moving energy from spirit into matter. However I choose to understand them, the Committee was the most unusual set of guides I have met. They certainly were real to my student, who has recorded pages of channeled material on a variety of topics.

For several years now I have watched relationships of trust and love develop between my clients and their guides. I have seen how being loved and protected by their guides comforts and strengthens my clients. I have seen them increase their personal power and self-expression by incorporating their guides' teachings into their lives. My experience has helped me truly to know the love and guidance available to us all, wheth-

er that guidance in fact comes to us from other parts of
our own consciousness or from independent beings.

Channeling Other People's Guides

Another important phase of my development as a
channel involved channeling other people's guides for
them. One of my first clients, Alan, a wise and gentle
man eager to pursue his spiritual development, felt
unsure of the direction this development should take.
During our second session, much to our mutual surprise, we both felt a presence in the room while we
meditated. I tuned into this presence and began to
channel Rashmar, a Taoist yogi, for him. Alan and I
worked together for a year. During that time, Rashmar
channeled hours of Taoist philosophy as well as spiritual initiations and specialized instructions to Alan through
me.

From the experience of channeling Alan's and other people's guides, I have learned that channeling
involves more than just a particular relationship between two beings—one in body and one discarnate. I
have learned that channeling as a function of consciousness can bring forth knowledge connected with
different times and places, that we can receive information or access the wisdom of beings whom we consider
dead. I now know that we can cross over into different
dimensions and receive information from beings very
different from us. The limitations of living in linear
time are only conventions, and we can transcend them
if we choose. Understanding that our consciousness
can access unlimited knowledge, and has unlimited
connectedness with all other beings, had provided me
with a great gift.

Working with Many Guides

When I first began to channel Diya, he told me
that I would form many spirit friendships and have
many teachers. This has indeed been the case. As I
have learned to contact many beings and many differ-

ent levels of consciousness, I have often utilized this ability to draw to me the teachings I desire. Although I do not currently work with Diya on a conscious level, I am aware in writing this book how profoundly he has affected me and how much his teachings and his love permeate my life.

Although the universe has been generous in providing guidance, my own discipline—finding time truly to incorporate these teachings—has sometimes been a problem. For instance, two years ago I wanted very much to learn how to heal with color. I prayed for appropriate guides to appear to teach me about color, and a set of guides did appear. After first giving me a basic primer on the esoteric meanings of the different colors, they asked me to commit an hour a day to learning to work with colors. Every day for weeks they had me practice tuning in to the colors that reflect aspects of the different energy centers of the body. But the exercises they assigned me, very much like piano scales in their repetitive nature, bored me. After about three months I found reasons to distract me from these teachings. I just didn't have the discipline to follow through.

In a similar fashion I asked for guides to teach me the path of Native American shamanism—practices that have interested me for years. I have managed to follow this path more faithfully. For several years I have brought groups of women together, teaching them how to use Native American rituals. During these sessions my guides have always come through and I have channeled a great deal of esoteric material. However, although I deeply love and respect this path and the teachers who have come to me, I still find it difficult to find the time to employ this guidance as much as I could. The difficulty does not lie in accessing different kinds of material. Once you learn to channel, the accessing is easy. But finding the time to integrate this material in a meaningful way may prove more challenging.

In the years since I first began channeling, I have learned to look at the universe as a vast library of information and consciousness—and at channeling as a kind of library card that allows us to go into the stacks. When I want to learn something, I call for beings or teachers to instruct me. I approach these guides with humility and love, recognizing the blessing of having other beings share their wisdom in this way.

Channeling the Higher Self

Another extremely important aspect of my channeling experience revolves around the higher self. Each of us has a higher self—a multidimensional existence unbounded by our current personality. Our higher self includes our current personality, but also incorporates our awareness of other incarnations and other levels of experience. Our higher self provides us with our link to the Great Self or God or All That Is. My guides have described the higher self as the mediator between our personalities and God. They say that if we truly merged with All That Is, our physical bodies would disappear. Our higher self acts as a mediator, allowing us to remain in body but at the same time to approach the total awareness of the Great Self. You may find it helps your understanding of this concept to recognize the higher self as a distinct being with its own intentions and qualities and evolutionary path. Our current personalities are just one specific experience that our higher self has created in order to learn certain lessons.

Perhaps you have undergone past-life regressions or have read books about past lives. People who explore their past lives gain access to the different experiences that the higher self has created in various learning situations.

I first recognized my ability to channel my higher self several years after starting to channel Diya. I began to notice that I had started to channel from a source that had a very different energy quality from Diya. Whenever I channeled Diya, I felt a heaviness and weight in my body; I never completely got over my feelings of exhaustion after channeling him. In addition, my word choice and grammatical structure always seemed stiff and formal when channeling Diya. Because a very different kind of consciousness was merging with my own consciousness, my system experienced this attunement as stressful and awkward. The new energy source that I began to notice, however, seemed very closely aligned with my personality. I could channel it for hours without tiring, and the perspectives offered seemed different but not alien from my own.

As I have channeled different beings over a period of time, I have come to recognize the presence of my own higher self in these interactions. I have channeled beings or energies with widely different viewpoints and widely different specializations, but I have come to recognize the unique texture and flavor of my own energy as it combines with other beings, and to recognize all channeling as a merging of my own higher self with other beings. In a similar way, when I have looked at my own and others' past lives, I have discovered a constant beingness or spirit, an essence that remains consistent despite many cultural and ethnic variations.

Many people believe that merging with our higher or multidimensional self—bringing that part of us into the physical body—provides one of the major goals of our lives on earth. I have not yet merged with my multidimensional or higher self. I still tend to pick up information and gain experience somewhat linearly. I can move into dialogue with guides or see my past lives intertwining with my current life, but I still tend to absorb only one dimension of experience at a time.

I believe that in due time a process of transformation will allow us to have greater union with our higher selves. I can sense a hidden wisdom in the way this union reveals itself in bits and pieces through past-life memories or through channeling experiences. And I believe that all of these brief glimmers are nothing more or less than a training and a prelude to a higher state of consciousness.

A Final Introductory Note

Channeling has given me many gifts. It has transformed my experience of the universe, of consciousness, and of my own nature. It has increased my feelings of being loved and protected, and my knowledge of how to live my life with truth and meaning.

Sometimes people ask me why channeling has re-emerged as a focus of national consciousness in recent years. I believe that just as individuals grow and reach for expanded understanding, so does the collective consciousness grow. People hunger for a deeper experience of themselves and life.

Channeling furnishes us with one path to explore consciousness. Channeling does not in itself provide the endpoint. It does not even offer the only way we can learn to see our own natures more fully. It is a tool or technique that can expand our awareness of our own multidimensional nature and our connectedness with all of life. From this new awareness, though, we can gain a great sense of meaningfulness and love in our lives.

I hope that you will benefit as greatly from this tool as I have.

Chapter One

Channeling Is for Everyone

Channeling is for everyone. Although everyone has this faculty, few of us ever become aware of using it. In this book you will learn to develop your own natural capacity to channel and use it to access wisdom and guidance that will enrich your life.

Channeling, Empathy, and Resonance

In its most basic form channeling is an act of empathy. As we live our daily lives, we experience many moments of spontaneous empathy where we briefly share the reality of another being. Our child falls off his bike, and we momentarily experience his shock and pain. A friend tells us of her plans to marry, and we experience her joy and excitement for a second or two. Someone tells us of the death of a friend we didn't know, and our eyes fill with tears. In each of these experiences we have registered the experience of another's reality and felt it in our own body and emotions. We have briefly channeled.

In most instances we fail to recognize these moments of empathy, covering them with our own thoughts, interpretations, and emotional reactions to the other person's experience. For instance, when our child falls off his bike, we may push aside our initial experience of his shock and pain, disguising it with our sympathy (feeling sorry for him), with our desire to take care of him, or with our own memories of falling off a bike. We quickly lose the initial experience of empathy.

When we intentionally channel, we expand and extend these moments of empathy. We put aside our own thoughts and reactions and allow ourselves to merge with another being for an extended period of time.

Channeling, of course, doesn't refer exclusively to relationships with spirit guides. Channeling is a particular state of receptivity and merging which can take place between any living things. By putting ourselves in a state of active empathy, we can channel plants, animals, our friends and families, dead relatives, highly evolved spirit guides, repressed parts of our personalities, or highly evolved parts of ourselves that we usually fail to recognize. Although this book concentrates on teaching you how to channel your spirit guides, it is important to understand that after developing this capability, you can apply it anywhere in your life.

I often use the word "resonance" when speaking about channeling. Resonance, a musical term, refers to the intensified and prolonged sound that occurs when the vibrations of different instruments are synchronized. Like an instrument, each of us produces a certain vibration or sound as the molecules inside us move in our own unique genetic pattern. All beings have their own vibrational frequency. When we merge with another in active empathy, our unique vibrations begin to synchronize and we resonate together.

Channeling depends on creating a state of active resonance with another consciousness, a relationship of active empathy that we can focus in any direction we choose. Our choice of direction will depend on our interests, our values, and what we need for growth and development at any given time. Hypothetically we could resonate to and channel many beings simultaneously. However, because we fear losing ourselves and we need to function in the physical world, most of us learn to channel selectively. If interested in animals, we may learn to channel animal intelligence. If we have a strong desire to heal others, we may attract healing energies which we can channel to the sick. If we want to learn spiritual principles and develop spiritually, we may in channeling find ourselves attracted to highly evolved spirit guides. Most of us learn to channel selective beings at selective times, but the skill of channeling creates the potential for union with all beings and with many kinds of healing energies.

Channeling and the Desire for Expansion

As you are reading this, you may wonder what gives channels the flexibility to set aside their own responses and interpretations so that they can channel another being. We all know how difficult it can be to change a habit or to admit another's perspective has more truth than our own. Given that we all tend to have such deeply ingrained ways of perceiving and acting, what allows us to channel?

Our own desire to expand our awareness plays a large part in enabling us to channel. At some point in your life you have probably had the experience of finding yourself in a situation where you hungered for another perspective. For example, in a work situation you may have found yourself going round and round trying to solve a problem. Finally frustrated by the repeated patterns of your own thinking, you turned to someone else for another perspective. Or in a personal situation when you felt bound by your own emotional responses, you may have needed advice or counsel to broaden your perspective.

The flexibility to channel comes from a desire to broaden our perspective and our perception. It comes from the realization that our conscious personality is comprised of an extended system of habits and responses that we have adopted in order to survive in the world. We begin to realize that we have locked ourselves in, repeating patterns of intellectual, emotional, and behavioral response. The desire to break out of these patterns and to perceive life in a new, fresh way provides the flexibility necessary to channel.

Channeling and Trance

If desire for expansion creates the emotional motivation to channel, trance or deep meditative states provide the proper atmosphere for channeling. Trance and channeling go hand in hand. Trance allows an individual to disconnect from the conscious personality—with all of its habitual responses, reactions, and interpretations. Trance allows us to create the state of openness and receptivity we need to resonate with and channel another being.

Because many different levels of trance exist, each individual must find the particular depth of trance he or she needs in order to disconnect from the conscious personality.

For example, as a *light-trance channel,* I remain fully conscious when I channel. Light-trance channels can listen to the information that passes through them and continue to experience the external environment as they channel. However, like all channels, they have temporarily turned away from the outer world and tuned into the inner world—where the five physical senses have less prominence. Light-trance channels may experience visions or feel different sensations running through their bodies as they channel. These sensations might consist of increased vibrations or subtle energies which move through their bodies, or they might feel various unexpected emotions. The techniques you learn in this book will prepare you for light-trance channeling.

Channels who use a *medium trance* hear only fragments of what they channel. They retain very little awareness of the world around them as they channel, and afterward remember little of what went on while the channeling was taking place. Medium-trance channels do not describe themselves as becoming unconscious during trance. Rather they say that they enter a different state of consciousness or awareness. Some describe it as a dreamlike state.

Deep-trance channels become totally unconscious during trances. Their personalities vacate the body, allowing another being to take control. Some deep-trance channels describe each channeling as an experience of death. Some deep-trance channels return to consciousness remembering dreamlike feelings, but these feelings have no particular imagery or content. Deep-trance channels often work in partnership with someone who will remain conscious while they channel. This partner takes care of the body for the channel and later lets the channel know what has transpired. Deep-trance channeling demands a good deal of trust and surrender, and working closely with a partner often helps the channel develop the trust needed to surrender in this way.

The depth of trance that each individual will need in order to channel depends entirely on his or her own personality. Individuals who find it difficult to let go of their own viewpoints may need to employ a deeper trance that will temporarily allow them to set aside their conscious personalities. Individuals steeped in religious or cultural conditioning that condemns channeling as harmful may need to use a deeper trance to overcome their resistance. Some individuals prefer lighter trances because they want ultimate responsibility for what they say; they feel that unconsciousness strips them of this accountability. Some individuals look forward to the break from their conscious personalities; they feel that unconsciousness enables them to merge with their guides in a deeper way. The depth of trance that you employ will depend on your own personal preference and the degree to which you feel attached to your conscious personality.

Channeling and Expression

Resonance, the desire for expansion, and trance are essential ingredients of the channeling experience. But channeling also requires the channel to express this resonance in some form. Of course, you can communicate with many kinds of beings without allowing yourself to express that connection. But this empathic resonance, called telepathy, is not channeling in the strict sense of the word.

From personal experience I know that I can carry on internal dialogues with my guides while driving, cooking, or cleaning house: this is telepathic rapport. However, when I sit down and allow my guides to express the same information through me, whether through the written or spoken word or any other medium of expression I choose, I am channeling. The resonance and the information received may be identical in both instances, but one situation involves telepathy while the other involves channeling. You may find it helpful to think of channeling as expressed resonance or expressed telepathy.

The form channels use to express this resonance varies greatly. Some of the options available to today's channels include music, dance, visual art, words, mathematics, and pure energy. The particular form I have chosen is words. As a primarily verbal creature, I express this energy mergence with words. Most of today's best-known channels are also verbal channels. However, words provide just one of many vehicles that channels can use to express resonance.

The famous Brazilian channel Luis Gasparetto has channeled thousands of paintings from the great European masters. Gasparetto goes into trance and produces canvases within three to seven minutes, painting with both hands and sometimes with his feet. He often simultaneously channels different artists—among them Degas, Van Gogh, Modigliani, Monet, and Picasso—through each hand.

You may have seen the Oscar-winning *Amadeus* several years ago. This movie portrayed the young composer Mozart as a coarse, narcissistic person. However, when he began to compose, an outpouring of complex, completed musical scores eclipsed his crass personality. Whether Mozart resonated to other beings, to his own higher self, or to some other energies, may remain unclear, but the creative process as depicted in this movie provides an excellent example of channeling.

Another type of channeling occurs in psychic healing. By surrendering themselves to what they regard as holy or sacred, psychic healers allow healing energies to come through them. Perhaps the best-known channel of these healing energies in Western culture was Jesus. The Bible contains many stories of how Jesus healed the crippled and the sick. However, Jesus did not have a patent on these abilities. All societies have given birth to individuals who could channel these energies. The movie *Resurrection*, featuring Ellen Burstyn, offers an excellent portrayal of a healer.

The Many Applications of Channeling

This book will focus on teaching you one form of channeling—interacting verbally with your spirit guides. However, remember that channeling can involve much more than this one application. In fact, I believe that channeling has re-emerged as a focus of public attention to teach us about the more universal use of resonance. We live in a world where we have learned to see many things as separate from us and as essentially dead. As such, we have learned to see the earth as a dead object, something we can exploit. We have learned to see our enemies as faceless others who lack a common humanity and aliveness. This way of looking at things has created a dangerously polluted world, one densely targeted with nuclear weapons.

Clearly we need a new way of thinking and behaving in order to survive. I believe that channeling will teach us how to merge energetically and create a bond of love with beings very different from ourselves. This ability to feel our essential oneness with all of life may play a crucial role in our survival; for it is impossible to kill or exploit beings that we are one with. I believe that someday soon we will be able to experience the active resonance of channeling with all beings; channeling spirit guides serves as a beacon, dramatically teaching us about the more universal applications of resonance and telepathic rapport.

The History of Channeling

Now that you better understand the essential nature of channeling, let's take a brief tour through history to see how this human capability has appeared over time. In particular, let's examine how different societies have channeled different energies and entities, depending on their unique worldview and interests.

Probably the first instance of channeling occurred in shamanic cultures throughout the pre-industrial world. These cultures used fasting, chanting, dancing, and sometimes drugs to induce trance. While in trance, individuals would merge with the spirits of animals to learn the specific powers of those animals. Shamanic cultures believed that every animal had special talents and skills for survival; by merging with a particular animal, one could absorb those powers and carry them back into ordinary life. The power of these animals was often channeled into dancing, where the channel would merge with an animal and let the animal spirit move his body.

Another prominent example of channeling occurred in ancient Greece, where specially trained channels went into deep trance and delivered messages from the gods. These oracles, connected with the temples of powerful gods, would channel verbal messages from the gods to the supplicant. Political and military leaders faithfully consulted with the oracles before making important decisions.

The eighteenth century produced Emmanuel Swedenborg, one of the most interesting channels in history. Swedenborg mastered nine languages and worked as an engineer and scientist in Sweden. His inventions included a submarine, musical instruments, an ear trumpet, and a fire extinguisher. At the age of fifty-six Swedenborg, the master scientist, turned inward to explore the inner world. He spent the last decades of his life in conversation with spirits and angels. He wrote:

> *The discourse or speech of spirits conversing with me was heard and perceived as distinctly as the discourse or speech of men; nay, when I discoursed with them whilst I was also in the company of men, I also observed that as I heard the sound of man's voice in discourse, so I heard also the sound of spirits each alike sonorous; insomuch that the spirits sometimes wondered that their discourse with me was not heard by others; for in respect to hearing there was no difference at all between the voices of men and spirits.**

The nineteenth century brought on a flourish of channeling activity and of scientific investigation of the channels (known as mediums). If today channeling seems focused on spirit guides and evolved spiritual teachers from other dimensions, the nineteenth-century mediums focused on channeling messages from the dead. Mediums such as the Fox sisters in the United States claimed to bring forward messages from the dead. In England a channel named Florence Cook reportedly had the ability to materialize the forms of various spirit guides who delivered messages from the dead. Cook's most commonly channeled spirit guide was Katie King, whom researchers claimed both to see and touch.

Researchers in both the United States and England formed societies for psychical research. Well-respected intellectuals such as William James, often regarded as the father of modern psychology, investigated and recorded hundreds of cases of reputed mediumship. The movement away from the limitations of materialistic thought, and the search for proof of dimensions beyond the physical world, had clearly begun.

Twentieth-century channeling has focused on

---

*Jeffrey Mishlove. *The Roots of Consciousness: Psychic Liberation Through Science, History, and Experience,* Random House, 1975, p. 55.

delivering spiritual messages and individual healings from highly evolved discarnate beings. Edgar Cayce, the Sleeping Prophet, went into deep trance to channel life readings and medical readings. The Association for Research and Enlightenment in Virginia Beach, which Cayce founded, has kept records of over 9000 of his readings. Cayce also channeled volumes of material on health, the lost continent of Atlantis, and potential spiritual and geological shifts for earth's future.

In the mid-sixties Jane Roberts began channeling an entity named Seth. Over a twenty-year period Roberts channeled volumes of material on the nature of personal and collective reality, on our multidimensional selves, and on the nature of creativity. Although her material came from an unusual source, it reflected a growing interest in personal creativity and metaphysics.

Today channeling has begun to flourish once again. Professional channels offer readings and workshops to ever-growing clientele. How to Channel Workshops are held throughout the country. Perhaps the most interesting aspect of contemporary channeling is its relatively democratic nature. Although certain "stars" have emerged on the channeling circuit, most trustwor-
thy channels will quickly point out that anyone can channel and that spirit guidance belongs to everyone. Whereas in many cultures channeling has belonged to an elite or to the exceptional, channeling in our times has been rediscovered as a capability that everyone has.

Whetting Your Appetite

By now I hope you have gained a basic understanding of and appetite for channeling. You can participate in this complex and varied phenomenon based on the development of empathic abilities we all share. You, too, can reach a state of active empathy or resonance by entering your most suitable level of trance and focusing your channeling efforts on anything from animals to highly evolved spirit guides who have never lived on earth. If you want to channel, you, too, can express your resonance with other beings and energies through a variety of forms, including words, art, and music—whichever you prefer.

I hope this introduction to channeling has whetted your appetite and excited you. Channeling, as a sensitivity and a capacity of consciousness that belongs to us all, is our birthright. It offers all of us a potential doorway to union with all beings.

Chapter Two

The Channels Speak

In the last chapter we reviewed some of the fundamentals of channeling. We explored channeling as expressed empathy or resonance that takes many forms and has many applications. We also looked briefly at the history of channeling.

In this chapter, four channels will share their experiences of channeling. Two of these channels—Sanaya Roman and Darryl Anka—are professionals who channel publicly. The other two channels—Joanna Bongiovanni and Thom Elkjer—integrate channeling into busy lives in other professions.

In interviewing these people I focused on practical matters rather than theoretical ones. I directed my questioning toward how channeling has affected their lives, rather than eliciting their theories about their experience. With this in mind I asked them five basic questions:

How did you begin to channel?

How does channeling fit into your life? How often do you channel? For how long?

How would you describe your relationship to your guide?

How has channeling affected your life? What have you learned from it?

Has channeling affected your view of the universe and your place in it?

As I interviewed these channels, I noticed many similarities in their experiences, despite the differences that grew out of their unique talents and their unique connections with their guides. I also noted how their experiences coincided or differed from my own. I have organized the interview material around themes, highlighting these differences and similarities in experience. The beginning of this section presents brief introductions to the channels and their guides.

Brief Profiles of the Channels

Sanaya Roman

Sanaya Roman, a thirty-seven-year-old woman who lives in Oakland, California, is a professional channel. She has produced a line of metaphysical tapes, and conducts workshops that teach people how to channel and reach expanded states of consciousness. She has published three books: *Living with Joy, Personal Power Through Awareness*, and *Opening to Channel: How to Connect With Your Guide*. She works in partnership with Duane Packer, a gifted healer and channel.

Sanaya has worked with her guide, Orin, for ten years. Like many high guides, Orin feels that focusing on who he is rather than on what he has to teach can only distract us from his message. However, he has described himself as a spiritual teacher who exists in many systems of reality besides those based on physical laws. He refers to himself as a researcher, reporter, teacher, and guide. Orin is intimately connected with Sanaya's professional life—her books, tapes, and workshops—in addition to serving as her spiritual teacher.

Thom Elkjer

Thom Elkjer, a thirty-one-year-old man who also lives in Oakland, works as a freelance writer for corporations and advertising agencies. He also writes plays, novels, and screenplays. Thom has been married for several years.

Thom and his guide, Mithra, have been working together for a year and a half. Their relationship, which consists of short, pithy teachings from Mithra, has led Thom toward increased psychological healing and spiritual understanding.

Like Orin, Mithra has said very little about who he is, except that he is involved with the physical dimensions of being without being physical himself. He describes his experience as "broad and mystical" and confesses that, like the Druids of the past, he "prefers to remain in the forests and mists rather than on the hilltops." He has told Thom to call him Mithra, but also made it clear that he has created that name only as a convenience for Thom's sake.

Joanna Bongiovanni

Joanna Bongiovanni, a thirty-six-year-old woman who lives in Los Angeles, California, owns an independent production company that produces film and television. She lives with her husband, a Latin American film director.

Joanna has been developing her psychic abilities for over ten years. Her first contact with guides came a decade ago, but only in the past two years has she begun to channel formally.

Unlike the other channels interviewed for this book, Joanna calls herself a "radio receiver" channel. She tunes into different guides depending on the type of information she wants to receive, rather than working consciously with one particular guide. Her guides have included Blunam, a primarily nonverbal presence who appears to her in a blue light; the Sisterhood, a group of Native American guides who teach the feminine path of wisdom; and the Erenyis, an extraterrestrial group whom Joanna can barely contact because of their high vibratory level.

Darryl Anka

A thirty-five-year-old man who also lives in Los Angeles, Darryl Anka has been an artist since he began to draw at age two. As an adult he has worked as a graphic illustrator for five years and a special-effects miniature builder for ten years.

Darryl's guide Bashar first contacted him fourteen years ago. Bashar says that he comes from the planet Essassani, located 500 light-years in the direction of the Orion constellation. Darryl currently travels throughout the world, publicly channeling Bashar and spreading his spiritual teachings. Darryl has also produced several audio and videotapes that present the channeled teachings of Bashar. *The California Connection*, a book by Bob Decard, details Bashar's basic teachings.

Darryl has a contract with Bashar to work with him for nine years. After this time he sees himself building a futuristic theme park that he has already begun to conceptualize and design.

First Encounters with Channeling

Although a couple of the channels I interviewed had extraordinary experiences as teenagers, none of them began to channel consistently until they were in their twenties or thirties. By that time many of the Seth books by Jane Roberts had been published, giving them a context in which to understand and develop their experiences as channels. In fact, all of the channels interviewed here deliberately set out to develop their capacities as channels. For most of them the development of these abilities involved a period of preparation and study.

Sanaya's first encounter with Orin came when she was in her mid-twenties. At that time she got together with a group of her friends to discuss the Jane Roberts books and began to contact discarnate beings with a Ouija board.

Orin first came into my life once a week on the Ouija board. He gave me and all the other people I was working with messages that were actually as-

*signments to do each week in order to enrich our
lives and increase our spiritual growth.*

But despite the ease of this initial contact, Sanaya
was not yet prepared to channel Orin herself—without
using the Ouija board as an intermediary. She needed
to work with another guide for three years before she
felt ready to channel Orin.

> *I couldn't seem to bring in Orin physically.
> His energy was very strong and I had trouble
> breathing. It was a friendly feeling, but felt like
> having too much energy in my body.*
>
> *And so, another guide worked with me for
> about three years. He had me exercise and do all
> kinds of things that would allow me to hold Orin's
> high vibration in my body. One day, after I had
> been listening to other people's meditation tapes, I
> sat down with a tape recorder and really went
> under. When I came to, I realized that I had
> channeled Orin. He had made a guided meditation
> tape for me that taught me how to become a better
> channel.*

After this first guided meditation tape, Orin created other channeled tapes, each of which helped open
Sanaya further to her connection with him.

> *Orin began to make tape after tape, each about
> twenty minutes in length. They were guided medi-
> tation tapes that took me into a state of deep
> relaxation and helped me think positively, open up
> to higher consciousness, and become calmer and
> quieter. I listened to the tapes—I loved them—two
> or three times a day. It became easier and easier for
> me to channel Orin. And as the connection grew
> stronger, I began to take my channeling out into the
> world more.*

Although Thom did not go through the same
extended period of preparation that characterized Sanaya's

introduction to Orin, his first encounter with channeling involved a deliberate choice, too.

> *The first time I ever saw anybody channel was when I attended a public demonstration by Richard Ryal. That was the first I had seen or heard of channeling. I was pretty skeptical, but his demonstration was really convincing. After that, I had a couple of experiences of having professionals channel for me. And then, two nights before it started, I was invited to a channeling class by the instructor. With no time to think about it or wonder what it might be like, I said yes. Two nights later I was in class. That was in January 1986. I'd say that the first time I really channeled, as I now understand it, was a month or so later. And I've continued to channel ever since.*

Other than exposure to other channels, Thom did not refer to any specific practices he employed to prepare himself for channeling. However, he did indicate that he had used psychotherapy and practiced meditative techniques and various forms of exercise for several years. From my perspective, these kinds of growth techniques, often constitute a kind of preparation, creating the openness that channeling requires.

Like all the other channels in this book, including myself, Joanna sought out the channeling experience as part of her ongoing path of spiritual development. During her college years she studied cross-cultural mythology and religion. After college she started to explore her own inner experience through various growth processes. In her mid-twenties she simultaneously felt her own intuition open and met her first channel.

> *I became aware of how much stronger my own intuition was in my life, and I became sympathetically attuned to people in my family who were three thousand miles away. I knew what was going on in very strange circumstances. And at that time I was also introduced to a new friend, a voice teacher who*

*channeled a being named Cheng. At first it was
really beyond my belief to be talking to this tiny
woman as she channeled the booming voice of this
Oriental entity. However, the more conversations I
had with Cheng over the course of ten years, the
more I realized that the information he offered was
very different from the worldly information that my
friend had—even though it definitely made use of
her knowledge and talents. Cheng told me that I
could develop my own psychic abilities, which I
knew I had. He said that someday I would channel
too. Well, I just laughed at that. It was too far
afield for me.*

In 1978 Joanna enrolled in a psychic development
class which greatly enhanced her psychic abilities.

*When I moved to California in 1978 I studied
with a teacher who was teaching people how to use
their intuitive powers psychically. I learned from
this six-week course how much I knew intuitively
and what a pleasure it was to receive visual information, because a lot of my information was through
visual images at that time. The main lesson I
learned was that I could trust myself as the instrument, that I could get out of the way of my higher
self and bring through information very clearly and
accurately.*

Joanna told me that she practiced psychic work for
several years, even developing a small clientele for her
Tarot readings, using the cards as a focus for her
intuition. Eventually she took another step toward
working directly with her guides.

*Another real turning point or corner for me
was that even after doing so much psychic work, I
still found myself a little bit skeptical. Like, here
was another Cheng and how would I like another
being inside of me, using my body? Because I had
other friends who would channel, and an entity*

*would come through their body, and it would be
very different energy from theirs; it could be unsettling
sometimes. But basically I learned that I could stay
grounded myself and still allow that other information in.*

Of the four channels interviewed, Darryl experienced the most extraordinary introduction to channeling. Unlike the others, Darryl had only a passing
knowledge and interest in metaphysics before he met
his guide in 1974. But two dramatic experiences quickly
changed his life.

*For me the biggest turning point was fourteen
years ago. On two occasions in the same week, with
friends present both times, we actually had very
close broad-daylight sightings of Bashar's spaceship
over Los Angeles. I didn't understand at the time
that this sighting was a way of tapping into my
subconscious memory to get me started on learning
the things I needed to learn to fulfill the agreement I
had made with them. But spurred on by the sightings,
I began doing research into metaphysical ideas.*

Like all of the channels in this book, except Thom,
Darryl then studied Jane Roberts's book in what I
would consider a kind of preparatory period.

*As the years went by and I started to do more
and more research, I eventually read books on
mediumship—particularly the Seth material from
Jane Roberts. And ultimately I was introduced to
several mediums. One of the entities who spoke
through the mediums offered to teach mediumship to
anyone who was interested. Now, even after all my
research, I took him up on the offer not because I
thought it was something I wanted to do. I had read
all the books I could, and I still wanted to learn
more about it. So I thought, well, if I go into class,
I'll learn more about it. I'll see something contemporary in action.*

When I was in that class, in a receptive state, under the guidance of the other entity, Bashar and his people made the mental connection with me telepathically. And as soon as the telepathic link was there, the memory of having made the agreement [to work with Bashar] came back—who they were, who I was to them, what the ship sightings had been about, dream encounters, and conversations that I had had with them that I had totally erased from my mind. It all came back to me, and I saw how everything in my life had sort of led up to that point, to get me to realize that I had made the agreement.

How and When Channels Contact Their Guides

As you will see as you read this section, channels contact their guides in a wide variety of ways. Some establish contact privately, some publicly, some in either situation. Some channels simply go into a light trance, remaining fully alert during their telepathic conversations with their guides. Other channels use a deep trance in which they retain very little rational or thinking consciousness. Some channels have daily contact with their guides, while others only channel once or twice a month. Every relationship develops its own unique structure, one that satisfies the needs of both the channel and his or her guides.

Sanaya channels Orin in a variety of contexts. In addition to channeling private readings for individuals and teaching classes where she brings Orin through, Sanaya makes guided meditation tapes for others, using material channeled from Orin. She also has contact with him when editing and interpreting material channeled from him for books. All of these channeling activities have focused on Sanaya's primary goal in her relationship with Orin: to serve other people by providing them with a direct experience of higher consciousness.

In formal channeling sessions, Sanaya, a conscious

channel, uses a medium trance. However, because so much of her life is entwined with him, Sanaya does not feel the need to channel Orin to have contact with him.

> *I channel [for myself] once every week or so, but I feel we're so connected that Orin's ideas and direction come through frequently as momentary insights and I don't have to formally channel. There's an ongoing partnership where I begin to know how Orin would think about something. I feel we're connected by higher telepathy.*

Thom, who enters a light trance but remains fully alert while channeling, contacts Mithra sporadically. When he's channeling a lot, he will contact his guide two or three times a week. But at other times he may go two months or more without channeling.

The form of Thom's channeling shifts. Sometimes he will sit down and formally channel, and sometimes Mithra contacts him much more spontaneously—either as a complete surprise or an immediate response to Thom's request.

> *Sometimes Mithra comes to me, just right out in plain sight. I'll be walking down the street and suddenly I'm channeling. And there's some voice there, his voice speaking. Other times I'll be in a deep confusion, I'll suddenly slide into a deep crisis or some deep discomfort, and I'll call on him.*
>
> *When he comes, I'm almost invariably out of doors and walking. There's something about that combination. I seem to be more relaxed then. However, if I want to contact him when I'm indoors, there's never a problem.*

Like Sanaya, Joanna goes into a medium trance to channel, most often while lying down indoors. Joanna channels once or twice a month, usually when contacting guides for others or when spending time with other people who channel. Although she finds channeling for herself "very nurturing," she seldom finds the time to fit it into her busy schedule.

Darryl, who employs the deepest trance of the four channels interviewed, reports that he rarely channels when he is alone. Like Sanaya, he contacts Bashar primarily in the context of a professional situation.

How Channels Experience Channeling

The metaphors used by the four channels to describe their actual experience when channeling varied greatly. For Thom, the experience most often seems conversational.

> When I channel, he speaks out loud. When it's conversational in a sense, it's not out loud. It's really distinct. It has all the quality of hearing somebody speak out loud, but the sound waves aren't there. It even feels like listening; it feels like physical hearing. There's the sense of information arriving just like when someone talks to you.

Darryl, however, who uses a deeper trance than Thom does, experiences waves of energy and imagery that he compares to the experience of listening to music.

> I am conscious, but not in the way that I am now. I'm conscious in a very different way. It's like being lost in a daydream state. What I receive in the trance state is so much more overwhelming in terms of the pictures and the emotions and the energy, that there's no thinking per se. I can't literally hear the words that are being said and think about them in a typically analytical, rational way. But I can feel the interchange going on. I know there's an interaction, but for me it's more like listening to music. You know how you can listen to a concert and get a sense of how the music moves you, and you could put a story or some idea to it. You could say that the way the music swells or changes can represent

*or call forth pictures within you that might make
conversational sense, but it's not like you can put
words to it. Again, it's like you were having a
daydream: If somebody walked into the room and
called your name, you wouldn't hear them because
you're lost in what you're looking at.*

Like Darryl, Joanna compares her experience of
channeling to an art form, except in her case it's not
music, but acting.

*I really enjoy it. Because I'm also an actress, I
love having another being speak through me. When
people ask me—and this is very important—what it
is like to do psychic work, I say, "It's really like
acting—the same process." Of course, a lot of the
people who ask me might be in the business. But the
thing is, you're just making your inner house
clean, creating space there and inviting another
entity, another source of wisdom, to make use of the
talents, the propensities, that you as an incarnate
being have. So I actually love being taken over—
actually, for me it's not so much a physical entity,
although I sometimes can feel a different vibration.*

In describing her experience, Sanaya used by far
the most spiritual imagery.

*It was like coming home for me. When I
channeled, it was the most peaceful, loving, and
compassionate experience that I had ever had. It felt
like I was being overshadowed by a higher presence,
the way people describe how they feel in prayer, a
feeling of being lifted up.*

Receiving Guidance

Each of the four channels I interviewed feels that
he or she receives spiritual teachings or lessons from
guides. Each reported a sense of being able to tap into
wisdom, guidance, and information that far exceeds

their normal awareness. This common thread holds true not only for these four, but also for myself and every other channel I have ever spoken to. Within this general framework, however, the form and the actual content of these teachings vary widely.

Except for Joanna, who, as noted earlier, employs a radio-receiver approach to obtaining guidance, each of the channels has an intensely personal relationship with a single guide. The lessons they learn come in a specific format through that particular guide. And each individual guide tends to adopt a distinctive format that will best suit the substance of his or her teachings and the needs of the channel.

Sanaya's lessons from Orin have come in different forms over time. The earliest teachings, which came through the Ouija board and then through a series of guided meditation tapes, focused on helping Sanaya open herself to channeling and experiencing higher consciousness in all areas of her life. They were designed to help her develop the states of relaxation and a level of physical fitness so that she could channel Orin.

More recently Sanaya has been working in close partnership with Orin to teach others how to channel. Much of her life is now devoted to bringing his teachings into the world. The form of his guidance is currently helping her grow spiritually, expand her potential, and navigate the many choices that arise in relationship to the work they do together. Orin uses their joint work as a focal point for Sanaya's own development. Sanaya told me how he has helped her expand her notions of what she is capable of doing and creating.

> I was trying to decide what to do next in my life, and I thought I would like to teach a class with Orin. When I asked Orin about it, he said, "Let's teach a class on the Spiritual Laws of Money. I really would like to help change the human thought forms around money. I'll help you put together a course." I had thought about having a simple class with three or four people. But Orin was talking

about changing the mass thought form around money! Orin thinks in much larger and more universal terms than I do. I thought, "I don't know anything about the spiritual laws of money," and I only had two weeks to put it together. But an inner voice said, "Trust. You can do it." So I put out a flyer announcing the class. And in two weeks, I channeled all the information I needed. It became the book Creating Money. *He took my original idea of giving classes, and out of it came a book.**

Thom's relationship with Mithra, like Sanaya's association with Orin, is extremely intimate and has involved specific lessons and teachings. However, in Thom's case these lessons have focused directly on furthering his personal spiritual and psychological healing, rather than involving a working partnership. In fact, Mithra refuses to allow Thom to channel him for other people unless the channeled material will be directly relevant to Thom's own growth. When I interviewed Mithra and asked him to tell me more about himself, he responded with extreme caution and eventually refused, maintaining that this information could not benefit Thom at this time.

Thom, a professional writer by trade, feels that he sometimes overcomplicates his understanding with too many words. With this in mind, he originally asked for a guide who could give him direct, focused guidance, and he has received just that.

> *There's generally not a lot of discussion. I asked for and met a guide who is not verbose. Probably the main kind of personality marker you could identify is short, pithy lessons or teachings, not the kind like, "You should tell Charlie that you don't want to do this job for him." It's much more like long-term lessons, teachings that last for years.*

---

*Thought forms in metaphysical understanding are the ideas and beliefs that precede and underlie our physical world. Mass thought forms are ideas and beliefs shared by a large group of beings.

Thom told me two examples of the kinds of lessons Mithra gives him: "A warrior is not divided against himself," and "Experience you're here." Once Thom has received a lesson, he works with it over a long period of time. The meaning of these lessons, he said, "Unfolds. It doesn't change, it unfolds. I understand it more, and it always has the quality that I knew what he meant all along and I'm continuing to discover how much meaning there was." The "Experience you're here" lesson unfolded this way for Thom:

> Well, it meant, when he first said it, that I just needed to stay grounded and in the moment. I thought he was just saying, "Get it together and bring attention to yourself." But after a year of working on that question and doing other things— meditating and thinking about my life—I recently rounded back on the idea and realized that I have a very large unworthiness complex, based on my childhood experiences. The way I began to deal with the pain of my childhood was to check out, to sort of leave or quit because the pain and conflict became overwhelming. And I realized that for me to make the things happen that I want, I'm going to have to realize that I'm not gone, that I'm here now and that I'm the one who is running the show. I'm here. And when I experience that, I'm able to summon energy and will.

Darryl's relationship with Bashar parallels both Thom's and Sanaya's with their guides in that he has received transforming teachings from a guide with whom he is intensely involved. However, while Thom receives highly personalized lessons and Sanaya's lessons combine highly personalized and more universal teachings, Darryl is presented with universal spiritual principles that he absorbs almost osmotically, applying them to his own life.

> As he makes telepathic connection and as he comes through to speak to other people, even though

I'm not hearing the conversations because I'm in an altered state of consciousness, I absorb the principles directly on an intuitive level. So all that information, all that knowledge, is within me. And I find that when I trust it and apply it, it comes out as it needs to. I find that I have the knowledge and the ability to apply that knowledge when and where I want.

This absorbed knowledge has given Darryl the ability to transform his life, redefining the direction of his own progress.

I think that the basic foundational teaching is that you do in fact create your reality. And I mean physically. All the physical experiences you have are the result of what you have been taught to think they are. Belief creates the experiences we have in life. Therefore I'd say one of the strongest principles to understand is that if you can get in touch with what your beliefs are, what you really believe about life, whether it's a conscious or unconscious belief, it will show you in no uncertain terms why certain things happen in your life. And if things happen in your life that you don't prefer, once you know what the underlying belief is, you can redefine it. You can live in that new mode, and living in that mode— according to the new belief you prefer to have—will actually create physiological changes in your life that will be more representative of the new belief. So across the board, you can apply that to almost anything.

Joanna's communication with her guides qualitatively differs from the other channels' relationships. Because she does not work intensely with any one guide, she has not received a systematic sequence of channeled teachings. Rather, she accesses a rich tapestry of viewpoints and perspectives, each with its own distinctive character.

When I first learned to channel, I created my body as a jug. [See exercise in Chapter Seven.] It

*was from a particular Mayan cult situation that I
didn't know about—the Quiche tribe. And then
later, about six months later, I came across an
anthropological book that talked about the Quiche—a
pre-Mayan civilization—and their sense of time and
the calendar. It was interesting because I had channeled some of that information long before I consciously
heard of that group of people.*

Joanna finds the richness and variety of working
with more than one guide extremely stimulating.

*I can go from channeling psychic dialogue
within myself, very oriented toward the present day
and the problems I'm having or other people are
having in their daily lives, to channeling actual
information and points of view from a cross-cultural
perspective that I wasn't even aware of.*

How Channeling Affects Channels' Lives

In the channels' descriptions of how channeling
has affected their lives, although each expressed his or
her own unique experience, certain themes recurred.
These benefits, which I certainly recognize from my
own channeling experience, include: a greater sense of
power, a sense of being loved and protected, a feeling of having a totally consistent, reliable friend, and
a feeling of increased effectiveness and purpose in

Before Orin came into her life, Sanaya knew she
wanted to contribute to the world situation in a meaningful way, but she felt stymied about the best way to
accomplish this goal.

*My relationship with Orin is definitely a part-
nership committed to world service. Before he really
came in strongly, I had been asking as one of my
affirmations to show me what I could do to make a
difference in the world. I had worked in office jobs*

and businesses, but I didn't feel like I was contrib- uting; it felt like there was something missing.

When Orin entered her life, he brought with him a definite understanding of the work that needed to be done, a job that Sanaya could fill. In focusing her efforts consistently on that work, he has helped her to gain a sense of meaning and purpose in her life.

It's been clear from the beginning that Orin wanted me to teach people to channel and open to higher consciousness. He wanted me to ask of ev- erything I did: "How does this empower the other person? How does it serve them?" For instance, if I were going to meet a friend, he would ask, "What do you have to offer them? How are we serving them by being with them?" He helped me see that everything I do should have a purpose: to serve and empower others. He gives me a bigger and bigger picture of the world and how I can help out.

With her new understanding of how she can con- tribute to the world, Sanaya's sense of personal power has increased dramatically. Thom has also gained a heightened sense of his own personal power through channeling. For Thom, though, this growth has sprung from the understanding that channeling has brought him about his psychological structure and about what he needs to heal.

I've been in therapy twice now—once for six or seven months and now for two or three months. And during both of those rounds of therapy, lessons from Mithra have been provided—very direct guid- ance on the issues I need to face, like not being divided against myself. That was what led me to understand that I had split off from myself at a very early age. And then the idea of experiencing that I'm here led me to understand how I could knit myself together again. Now those are psychological disorders, but it was these very direct lessons that

*expanded my understanding of myself, that gave me
new understanding.*

Through Joanna's channeling experience, she has
gained a much greater self-confidence in her work.

> *It's not direct. It's not the same as painting
> and drawing. That's a direct channeling. But the
> way it helps me, well, what it all comes down to is
> self-confidence. There are so many issues in my
> work, so many decisions that have to be made in a
> split-second about people and things. I mean, there's
> so much combat and all that, that I think that
> channeling and psychic work have really helped me
> to trust my instincts and go on to the next thing.
> You know, if I have a feeling about something, I
> don't feel I have to justify it to myself.*

Darryl, too, feels that channeling has enhanced his
personal power and increased the effectiveness with
which he lives his life.

> *My life has gotten simpler, much more happy,
> much more effortless, much more automatic. The
> things I need just wind up being there when I need
> them. Things are clearer in terms of how one event
> might connect into another. There are always new
> things to learn, but there aren't the deep mysteries
> of life anymore. There are not as many burning
> unanswered questions on what's it all about, that
> sort of thing. I basically understand that being who
> we are to the best we can be is our fundamental
> purpose in life. And this allows me, or has allowed
> me, to begin to function in a simplified manner, and
> not to think that life is something I have to fight or
> struggle through.*
> *I've come to understand that the basic princi-
> ples are so simple, and there are really just a few of
> them. And once you understand them, then almost
> any question you come up with can be applied
> within that framework. So it's not like you have to*

keep coming up with a new principle for every question. If you remember the ten basic principles, then you have a tool that you can just apply and continue with your life.

Of the four channels I interviewed, all except Darryl volunteered that channeling has created an extraordinary sense of being protected and watched over in their lives. Sanaya eloquently expressed an increased love she feels in general due to channeling, a feeling that many channels, myself included, share.

> *Since I've been channeling, I've also found that my environment has become much more nurturing. Through channeling I've learned to accept and receive love. Orin is so much love, that to channel him, I've had to open to love and being loved. So, my own caring for other people has greatly expanded.*

Closely connected with her expanded capacity to care for others has been a shift in Sanaya's perception that is directly attributable to her relationship with Orin.

> *When Orin tunes into people, he has such caring and compassion that I have learned to see people not for their outer personality but through his eyes, where they're all beautiful beings. I've learned to see their souls more. I don't get so caught up in "They work in this or that job" or "They've got a personality that bothers me" or "They've got a beautiful personality that might catch me." Through Orin I can see their souls and everyone is so beautiful.*

How Channeling Affects Channels' Views of the Universe

Each of the channels I interviewed echoed my own feeling that channeling has not only transformed our perceptions of ourselves. The universe has shown itself to be much richer than we had ever imagined. At the same time, it appears more ordered and meaningful and safe.

Darryl told me about the abundance that channeling has opened him to.

> *I guess that what I've learned through intuition is that the universe is perhaps far richer than any of my analysis allowed me to realize. Not that you cannot through reason understand its richness. But I think that the intuitive side puts you more strongly into an experiential relationship with that richness and with all the possible realities that can be. It's very different from just knowing, okay, there could be a lot of possible realities, but not necessarily feeling that any one of them could be real to you.*

Joanna's viewpoint, which also recognizes the enormous possibilities inherent in the universe, closely mirrors Darryl's:

> *It's really opened up everything. Everything is up for grabs. I just have to accept that there are many simultaneous histories and lives and viewpoints. I think channeling has opened the universe up. I am not into past lives per se. I don't know anything about whether they exist or not. I'm not into extraterrestrial UFOs. But I accept them. I haven't experienced them and I don't accept them blindly, but it's absolutely viable to me that there are other cultures in the universe.*

Thom identified the expansion that he has felt in more personal psychological terms.

> *I would say that channeling has radically changed my sense of the world as a place where I belong and where I can have dreams and make them come true. I didn't really experience the world in that way before. But there was something about the quality of calling for a guide in a particular kind of relation-*

ship, calling for a particular kind of help and not only getting it, but getting it beyond my expectations and my understanding. It's like the universe is giving me a gift so big that I can't even see it except in small doses. And that makes me feel that some other kinds of things are possible—like there's hope.

Sanaya's changed view of the universe echoed Thom's in that she also feels more hope. By seeing the guidance available to humankind, she feels an increased sense of hope, safety, and personal power.

Channeling has given me more hope. I see how much work is being done in the higher realms to protect mankind, because there really is a tremendous amount of caring. It's also given me a feeling of safety, an understanding that it's not as random as we think out there. We're not at the mercy of these random forces. Because we have guidance and assistance out there that really works, I feel much more personally empowered and I feel the universe is safer. Before it seemed like, "Maybe you get lucky and maybe you don't." But now it feels like if you tune in, you can tap into higher dimensions and you can utilize that power to get results. I don't mean using it in a negative way. You can utilize that power to make a difference in your own life.

A Brief Note to the Reader

Hopefully, in reading the words of these channels, you have gained an appreciation for the richness and the variety of the channeling phenomenon. Although the general process called channeling always involves moving beyond one's normal personality and consciousness and resonating to other beings and other levels of consciousness, within this general process the individual experience of channeling still allows for a great deal of diversity. The types of guides attracted, the nature of the relationship between guide and channel, the state of consciousness the channel is in when receiving guidance, and the ways of integrating channeling into one's life vary from channel to channel.

As you move into your own unique relationship with your guides, despite these individual variations, you *can* expect to share certain experiences with the four channels interviewed here, with myself, and with most of the channels I have met. You can anticipate receiving new perspectives and perhaps systematic teachings and lessons from a high spiritual being or from higher aspects of your own self. Your view of the nature of the universe will certainly expand, and you will experience a new sense of order and meaning within that richness. Finally you can expect to feel loved and protected. In the diverse world of channeling, these are shared realities.

Chapter Three

The Guides Speak

After reading the channels' perspectives on the relationships they have with their guides, you probably have many questions about the guides themselves. When I first met Diya, I, too, wondered what the guides were like. In getting to know Diya and various other guides, and in contacting the guides of the four channels interviewed in Chapter Two, I have learned much more about their nature. In this chapter, I will share what I have learned: who the guides are, how they come to work with specific humans, what they teach, and what they gain from their interaction with human beings.

Who Are the Guides?

When I began to channel Diya, he told me that there are four primary types of relationships between humans and nonincarnated beings. Because my own experience has verified this typology, I am including it here.

Channeling Relationship: Type 1
According to Diya the first kind of relationship between channels and their guides exists mainly for entertainment.

Just as some human beings drift along without consciously evolving, there are also entities who just "drift" between incarnations. These nonincarnated beings often get bored, and they enjoy parlor games with humans just as humans do with them. Diya says that most beings who communicate through the Ouija board are this playful type, although occasionally a highly evolved entity may employ this same means to approach a channel.

Personally, I have found the beings that come through a Ouija board either unpleasant or trivial. Usually these beings have not completed their earthly lives and have been unable to make the transition to another level of consciousness. During my early twenties I had my most memorable contact with these frivolous beings. My friends and I were playing with the Ouija board in a house in Rhode Island. A being came through who claimed that, while trying to retrieve gold from the basement of the house, he had been killed in a house fire on that site. He seemed very surly, and somewhat obsessed with blaming his problems on Andrew Jackson, whom he considered a scoundrel. This being spoke through the Ouija board for hours, exhausting the channel, who, despite being double blindfolded, moved the plaquette from letter to letter at amazingly rapid speeds while in trance. Although I was fascinated by the phenomenon, I found this being quite unpleasant and decided I was not interested in pursuing more contact with his kind.

Generally speaking, I don't try to channel deceased relatives or friends. Just being dead doesn't make one a desirable guide. In fact, beings that hang around for contact usually do so because they lacked resolution in their earthly lives, or they fail to understand clearly that they have now moved on to another dimension of experience.

Channeling Relationship: Type II

Diya described a second type of relationship that exists between humans who want to learn and nonincarnated entities who have chosen teaching responsibilities as a phase of their growth between lifetimes. These relationships usually arise between beings who belong to the same soul group, or beings who are part of the same entity.

Diya believes that we are all multidimensional beings who have many simultaneous experiences, some of which we call past lives. We create simultaneous lives with beings who are compatible with us in intention and in basic energy frequency. And we create these realities with the same beings, who all belong to our soul group, again and again. In saying that many channeling relationships involve members of the same soul group, Diya means that communication still continues even though not all members of the soul group have taken physical form in the same time-space reality. This continued communication sometimes takes the form of channeling.

This type of teacher/student relationship, as Diya mentioned, may also take place between beings who are part of the same entity. In these instances, we communicate with parts of our own multidimensional self that are incarnated in different times or that are not incarnated at all.

Much of the guidance that channels receive from beings who are distinctly human but not currently in body comes through this type of relationship. These beings may bring the teachings of specific spiritual paths: Hindu, Taoist, Buddhist, Christian, Jewish, Muslim, Native American. Or they may be prosaic guides—Joe or Sam—who teach wisdom in simple ways. They often have an ethnic or cultural heritage very different from the channel's own. But despite this variety, the common trademark of these guides is that they are clearly embarked on the human path of evolution. Relationships with them further the development of both the incarnated being and the guide, and by disseminating the channeled words to others, the channels can help many people expand their understanding.

Channeling Relationship: Type III

A third sort of relationship occurs with nonincarnated beings who follow a non-human evolutionary path.

Diya has indicated that millions of different kinds of conscious life exist throughout the universe. Interaction between different types of beings involves mutual expansion as each type learns about the functioning of the other. This type of relationship is most beneficial to highly intellectualized human beings, for the encounter tends to set their intellectual notions upside down. Despite this intellectual upheaval, however, the channels can still acquire valid and useful wisdom, for the principles of love and compassion are the same for all kinds of beings. Darryl Anka has this kind of relationship with his guide, Bashar, who comes from a nonhuman civilization and is on an entirely different strand of evolution. Bashar does teach universal principles of creativity, but he has also opened the window to different possibilities by describing his culture to Darryl.

Channeling Relationship: Type IV

A fourth type of relationship arises between humans and entities whose evolution is unconnected with the lessons of being in any particular kind of form.

Diya is this type of entity. He describes himself as an overmind whose job involves overseeing the development of many kinds of species. He himself does not have a body of any kind but is rather a complex structure of consciousness. Diya has given me several analogies to help me understand his nature. He once likened himself to a vast computer without the hardware. Another time he told me to imagine sitting in a drive-in theater with millions of screens of experience all around me. This image, he said, is analogous to his experience.

Channeling Relationship: Type V

I would like to add a fifth type of guidance relationship unmentioned by Diya, one between two incarnated beings who have no physical contact with one another.

It is well known that the great East Indian yogis taught their disciples from afar. I myself have learned many of the teachings of Native American shamanism through teachers who are currently alive, but whom I have never met. I have learned these teachings by bringing together a group of people and receiving channeled information from these beings in ritual and celebration.

Where Guides Come From

Often people ask me where guides live, what their worlds are like. Because some guides willingly share this information, while others refuse, I know of no detailed channeled material that addresses this question. Many guides feel that this kind of information can only distract us from the spiritual transformation we must focus on to survive as a species. There is, therefore, no precise cosmology of the universe that I can draw or that any other channel I know can draw. We do know, however, that if the guides are authentic, the universe teems with conscious intelligence. A few descriptions of these other dimensions follow. As you read about them, however, keep in mind that they represent just a small sample and do not indicate anything about an ultimate cosmology.

Guides on the human path of evolution but between incarnations describe their world as similar to ours in that beings exist in relationships and social groupings. These beings devote themselves to learning and spiritual growth in a much more conscious way than we generally do. The biggest difference between their world and ours is that theirs does not have dense materiality. Thoughts are actions, and things can be created or destroyed with thought. For instance, these entities can change their physical form or their surroundings with thought. They don't have to transfer ideas to matter. These beings, all linked telepathically, inhabit a world similar to ours in its goals and its creations. However, because their world is not materially bound, it is generally more refined than ours.

Guides from other civilizations have sometimes described their worlds. For instance, Bashar says that he comes from Essassani, Place of the Living Light. His planet, located five hundred light-years away, resembles our planet in that it has air and water, although the light on Essassani is green. Like Earth, Essassani has many plants and animals, but the animals can communicate telepathically with Bashar's race, and unlike animals on our planet, do not fight with one another to secure and maintain territory. As Bashar describes it, all the creatures of Essassani share their world peacefully and harmoniously. His race, which also communicates telepathically, has obviously advanced much further technologically and spiritually than we have.

Some people who have had contact with angels or light beings reported hearing beautiful music and seeing vibrant colors; in general, they do not describe the pearly gates depicted in Christian cosmology. From these accounts we know that these beings do not presumably live in civilizations or cultures, at least as we understand those words.

Perhaps the most apt analogy that I can make from my current understanding is to liken the universe to an enormous pulsating mind. This mind reverberates with many ideas and creative expressions of itself. We call these different ideas beings and entities. In the same way that the ideas in our human minds vary—applying to different levels of our experience, each with its own unique quality and textures—the many beings of the universe live in different dimensions of experience, each with its own distinct qualities.

How Guides Come to Work With Us

Guides primarily come to work with us in two different ways: through pre-incarnational agreements or in response to our conscious request. When we are physically born, we enter this incarnation with certain intentions and purposes. To accomplish these goals, we may make an agreement to work with certain guides during the course of our lifetime. These agreements are based on the guide's needs and goals as well as ours. Once we have come into a body, we may choose to honor this agreement or not, depending on later decisions we make in our lives. Orin described his pre-incarnational agreement with Sanaya this way:

> Our relationship to the channel is very much connected to our relationship with all of our work. As guides, we usually have our own agreements as to the energy we want to shift, as to how much we feel we can make a difference in increasing consciousness and bringing more light into the area we're working on. We work with the channel—usually from birth—at least my relationship with Sanaya has involved watching over her. Many have seen it to be like a guardian angel. Knowing that she may or may not reach upward and make the connection, we have begun working at an energy level should she want it, because at a soul level there has been an agreement to do this. She has asked to be guided from her birth, and we worked together before she came into this incarnation. Part of her challenge and growth opportunity in this lifetime was to serve other people. So we had very similar intentions prior to her incarnation. And we began to link up with her prior to her incarnation, with an agreement at the soul level that our work was very similar.

Mithra also implied that his relationship to Thom was longer and more profound than the one recognized by Thom's conscious personality.

> There is a longer thread, a quality of long-shared history and mutual understanding. I do not say this about the personality that is known to him or to others. I speak of the essential nature. All

*aspects of creation are evolving. There is no com-
pleted state as we would understand it. So the
nearest thing we can have in common is a sharing
of the pathway, of the process of evolving. There is a
natural selection, if you will. The request that
Thom made for a guide found me very quickly. So
our initial contact was only a matter of acknowledg-
ing what already was.*

Bashar's explanation of his relationship with Darryl
comes as the most surprising, because it challenges our
traditional notions of time and space. Bashar told me that
Darryl is actually a past self of his, a part of his multidimensional being sent to earth to explore our particular
reality. They made a pre-incarnational agreement that
Darryl would remember this relationship and would make
it available to others as a channel. Not only does this
allow Bashar to share his wisdom with us, but, as Bashar
describes it, the relationship also provides him with a
greater comprehension of our world and our experience.

*Recognize that in one frame of reference it can
be understood as a reincarnational relationship in
the sense that the channel is my past self, and
therefore provides for me and my civilization an
experiential model, a frame of reference through
which we may look and understand your civilization. Without this model, it would be unlikely that
our terminologies, our concepts, would fit very
neatly into your concepts at all, so alien would we
be to each other. But in having lived one life, so to
speak, upon your planet, it has given me a frame of
reference to understand many of the terminologies
and experiences—emotionally, mentally, and physically—that you have upon your planet, so that I
can be of help to you at this time.*

What the Guides Teach

As you might guess, the wide variety of guides
produces a wide range of information. Some guides

bring highly technical or scientific information, while others offer medical information or teachings about spiritual healing. Some guides convey the perspective of spiritual disciplines such as yoga or Native American shamanism. Others supply the viewpoint of an alien civilization looking at ours.

Although the guides exhibit much diversity in what they teach and in the characteristics they display in teaching, several recurring ideas have been expressed in almost every channeling that I've ever heard or have ever given. The ideas included here form a spiritual or philosophical context that all evolved beings seem to share.

1. Consciousness in the universe continually evolves, moving toward higher levels of compassion and unconditional love.

2. Many different kinds of life are conscious and involved in the process or evolution. Beings who have developed beyond us, and parts of ourselves that are more conscious than our personalities, can guide human beings in their evolution.

3. The earth is currently at a critical point in its development. Between now and the year 2011 we will witness a major shift in values, life-styles, and spiritual orientation as we move into greater spiritual maturity.

4. To reach this stage of greater maturity, the earth will need to undergo a major purification of existing values and social organization. Major changes in the earth itself—such as earthquakes and volcanic activity—may accompany these changes.

5. Many guides have now made themselves available to help us through these changes and enter a new age of harmony and world peace. New energies of a higher frequency are currently pouring into our world. However, as these energies interact with us, they may cause psychological and social unrest.

6. The human being is one part of a multidimensional soul or god-self. We are much, much more than we think we are.

7. We create our own experience on all levels of reality. There are no victims. If we create a difficult situation for ourselves, we do so in order to learn certain experiential lessons.

8. Matter follows thought. Our physical reality is created and shaped by our beliefs. To change our physical reality, we first need to look at our beliefs about what we want to change.

9. Although our individual expression demonstrates much diversity, we are all ultimately and in essence one.

As we saw in the last chapter, guides provide specialized instructions for their channels. However, the general principles listed above almost invariably underlie all of these individualized teachings.

What Guides Gain from Their Relationship with Humans

All of the guides I interviewed—indeed all of the guides I have ever met—indicated that they receive two main benefits from working with humans: the pleasure of serving, and the expansion of their own understanding and knowledge. Orin, Sanaya Roman's guide, spoke of the joy that he personally derives through serving others.

> *Our connection to the planet is to serve at a time of great transition. We are holding a focus of light for the many people who are making the transition and accepting the challenge of utilizing the higher energies that are coming in. Some people will experience it as a time of letting go. Other people will experience it as a time when they make a quantum leap. I am here to work with those who are*

*accepting the challenge of staying here on the planet
and making a shift.*

*We do experience great joy, and joy is so much
more immense than you feel just in the emotional
body. It is an expansion of our energy. It is an
increase of our own consciousness, our own ability.
What is truly left is service. This is one of the
greatest honors in our realm. You honor people
when they become president. We honor our beings
by allowing them the opportunity to shift and help
many people. It is a great responsibility and honor
because one must have mastered many levels, just
as your gurus must have mastered much of themselves.*

The Sisterhood, one of Joanna Bongiovanni's many
guides, talked about service in terms of the pleasure
they get in passing on truthful communication.

*Quite simply, we receive the opportunity to
communicate and pass on consciousness. There are
so few opportunities to pass on what is useful, what
is eternal, and most of all what is empowering for
an individual, for a race, for a culture; forget a
race—for a world community. How often do two
people of the same culture get to explore their values
and true speaking, let alone people and beings of
different cultures? It does not matter whether we
are entities who are passing on knowledge from one
culture to another, or whether we are shedding light
on daily domestic problems which our channel's
associates are experiencing. The truth, or the important thing, is that we are empowering the truth
within ourselves and the truth within you. We are
empowering you to true knowing, so that the power
you call intuitive, or the unconscious that links
each individual with the great beyond, is expressed.
So, truly, the value of our contact with you is
empowerment and the expression of truth.*

·Just as human beings speak of learning new perspectives and gaining understanding through channel-

ing, the guides refer to a similar process. When I first began to channel Diya, I asked him what the guides receive from the channeling experience. He replied that although many species are more advanced in their navigations of the inner worlds, few species are capable of traveling in both the inner worlds and outer physical worlds. For many beings, because they lack their own physical senses, the richness of our sensory worlds can seem very alluring. When they resonate with us, they vicariously enjoy an experience very foreign to their own.

Bashar, Darryl Anka's guide, also shed some interesting light on how guides expand through their contact with us.

> We as a civilization, and I personally, retrieve from this experience an awareness and an understanding of the different ways that different civilizations can express themselves, can express their creativity—particularly in the transformational age that your planet is going through—and the different manifestations of limitation that you have experienced for many tens of thousands of years in your society. This gives us a greater understanding of all the different ways that creation can manifest itself, and in learning more about you, allows us to apply this understanding to many other civilizations going through similar transformations as well.
>
> Therefore, in seeing all these different methodologies coming from such a highly focused, experiential planet in physical reality such as your own, we are treated to more expansiveness of the universe, because we see that there are that many more ways that infinite creation can manifest itself, and this expands our understanding of what the universe is and what creation is within us.

Mithra, Thom Elkjer's guide, views this expansion from a slightly different perspective. Whereas Bashar emphasized his increased understanding of different cultural expressions of the creative life energy, Mithra emphasized the expansion that comes from the blending of the essential nature of different beings.

> *There is a quality in the essential nature of all things that desires reconnection, desires to be reunified, for all things are essentially the same. This is at the heart of the devotion that people feel for their religious leaders or teachers, for there has been a contact made between their essential natures, and this is experienced as devotion. This devotional quality of essential natures recombining would be an accurate description from this side of the relationship.*
>
> *This recombining process continues with all beings on all planes at all times. It is a process that you have sometimes called alchemical. That is, it seems to include physical processes that are not physical. As far as working with other beings in this way, the relationship with Thom is unique, but then, all relationships are unique.*

A Final Word from My Guides

As I sat trying to decide how to end this chapter, I felt the familiar light-headedness and pressure in my head that tells me that my guides want to speak to me. When I tuned into them, they said that, since I have called this chapter "The Guides Speak," they would like to conclude it. I have worked with these guides for about a year, but they have never given me an identifying name, because they don't feel it is relevant to discuss their personal experience with me. These guides always begin their sessions with their identifying signature: "We are with you. We are always with you." As you read this short message, you will notice that its content very closely parallels what I described earlier as essential guided teachings.

> *We are with you. We are always with you. We wish to say that this is a time of great unfolding*

upon your planet, a time when old forms will rip open so that new life can present itself. There is an implied destruction of old forms as well as an implied bursting forth of new energies. Always in the process of growth, there is energy expended to allow the new life to break through the old containing structures that restrict and that belong to an earlier phase of development.

As you move through the changes of the earth's cycle in the next fifteen to twenty years, it is important to remember the lessons of growth that you see around you in all life forms. For the young sprout to break through the earth covering requires energy and a pushing against the resistance of the earth. The earth which was once a protection against the winds of winter is now an aggressive force which must be broken through so that the young plant can reach toward the sun.

In the same way, many of the earth's institutions have been like a protective covering for the young sprout of your consciousness. Now you as a race are ready to push beyond these protective institutions and to extend your souls toward the great sun of spirit. This is the time of a great unfolding and of a great push upward for your people.

As you see social changes, as you see old institutions crumbling, know that this does not represent the end of the world. Rather it represents the beginning of a new era of enlightened living.

Many are here to help you into this new era. You are loved. You are guided. If you remember the image of the young plant pushing through the confinements of the earth covering, you will be eased in the coming changes.

Thank you for letting us speak.

Chapter Four

Encountering Doubts and Resistances

As you read the accounts of channeling presented earlier in this book, you might have found yourself experiencing various degrees of skepticism. You might have wondered how people who sounded so sane could have slipped into such delusion, or questioned how such deluded people could still be considered sane, or suspected some kind of fraud in their stories or in my reporting.

The most effective and pertinent response that I can make to this kind of skepticism is this: try it for yourself and form your own opinion based on what you experience. Read books of channeled material and see if the wisdom they offer coincides with your own deep sense of truth. Go to see a professional channel and use your own knowledge and discernment to assess his or her authenticity. And most important, when you feel ready, try to develop this skill yourself; then make a judgment based on your own honest exploration of the experience.

The word skeptical is derived from the Skeptos Society, which existed during the Golden Age of Greece. The Skeptos Society dedicated itself to looking at all sides of an issue in a challenging, disbelieving manner. In examining any issue, these original skeptics refused to honor any assumptions or prejudices. Understood in this sense, skepticism is healthy. It keeps you looking for the truth in any situation and prevents you from being lulled into unquestioning prejudice.

If you have a truly skeptical attitude about channeling, then you will create your own experience to help determine whether guides exist or not. You will make your own judgments based on experiential inquiry into the phenomenon. If you use your own experience as a yardstick, you will be exhibiting true skepticism. If, however, you are not willing to explore this experience at all, then you are really just holding a bias.

Many years ago I took a lot of pride in my resistance to spiritual matters. I watched my friends "fall" right and left into Eastern spiritual movements and spiritual communities. I regarded their new spirituality as a weakness, an inability to cope with modern life. I prided myself on not sharing their weakness. But in truth, I wasn't skeptical, I was prejudiced. Although I had never really explored the realities my friends were speaking about, I made some pretty strong judgments and assumptions about their lives and values. However, because my views coincided with the dominant worldview of my culture, I could get away with feeling proud of my prejudice and my lack of true experience. I still have many biases and unwarranted assumptions, but I have learned to recognize them as prejudices, not as healthy skepticism.

My bottom line about channeling and skepticism is this: channeling really might not be your way or your path in the world. Many different paths may lead to expanded consciousness. However, choosing another path does not justify prejudging something that you have never really explored.

If at this point the accounts in this book have piqued your curiosity, and if you are willing to move ahead and explore this capacity in yourself, you might still find yourself encountering doubts and resistances in place of your initial skepticism. Every channel I know has encountered certain common resistances.

Although it is quite natural to feel such doubts, they can only stand in the way of your ability to channel. Putting them aside is the first step necessary to prepare you for channeling.

Doubt #1: *What If I Can't Do It?*

The first major doubt which you might encounter concerns your own ability to channel. "What if I can't do it?" you may ask yourself.

Almost everyone, including trained psychics, shares this doubt. What's more, much of our cultural conditioning supports this fear. Most people in our culture learned at a very early age to regard access to the unseen as a special gift that belongs to unique sons of God (Jesus, Moses, the prophets, Buddha, Mohammed) or to their representatives (the Pope, saints, or priests). We were taught that to reach beyond the veil of the visible, one must be special or chosen. As you have already seen in this book, this is not true. Ordinary people have learned how to connect with their guides and their higher selves and to experience subtle inner realities.

Another aspect of our conditioning, our scientific training, has also strengthened this doubt. Most of us, even if we have never formally studied science, have been strongly affected by this worldview. Science teaches us to judge things as real only if they can be measured and quantified by the five senses, and if other people, by using their five senses, can verify our own experiences by duplicating them under the same conditions. The scientific method determines truth based on physical data that can be analyzed and dissected. This relegates nonphysical realities to a state of nonexistence, by scientific standards. As long as we religiously cling to the scientific model, we will be unable to contact our spirit guides or open ourselves to subtle nonphysical realms of existence, because our definitions of reality will deny their existence.

Although part of you is probably very excited about the possibility of contacting your spirit guides, part of you may also doubt their existence. This conflict often translates into the feeling that you may not be able to do it at all. How could you contact nonexistent beings?

Caught between science, which tells you that the spirit world doesn't exist, and religions that tell you that it exists but is inaccessible to you, you may think, "I can't do it." *But you can.* If you are open and receptive to it, channeling is actually a simple skill.

Doubt #2: *Am I Going to Be Overwhelmed?*

You may also need to confront the fear that, "I'm going to be overwhelmed by this spirit entity." Variations of this are, "What if I lose myself?" or "I'm afraid that my guide will control me."

Again, these fears spring from our childhood conditioning. How many Grade B horror movies have you seen in which an evil spirit takes over someone's body and wreaks havoc on their lives and the lives of those around them? Yet in all my years of channeling and observing other channels, I have never seen or experienced anything remotely like the scenes portrayed in horror movies. As I mentioned in Chapter One, unconscious channels will sometimes experience shaking or twitching during their transition to channeled personality. Often the being that speaks through the channel has different voice patterns or accents, or the body language and worldview may contrast sharply with the conscious personality of the channel. Looking at this as an outsider, you could become afraid of being taken over if you decided to channel.

If viewing the changes that have happened to an unconscious channel has scared you, keep in mind that a contract always exists between the guide and the higher self of the channel about the form that the channeling will take. A guide will never take over in this way without the channel's consent. Unconscious channels often need this kind of eclipse of their personality to allow their guides to come through. Sometimes channels contact guides for other people who need to see this kind of dramatic eclipse to believe in the reality of spirit guides. The point is: whenever channels have agreed to become unconscious, they do so for a reason. They have chosen this course and are not being arbitrarily overwhelmed.

If you learn to channel consciously, as this book teaches, you need not feel afraid of losing autonomy or control. You will always have the opportunity to decide whether you feel comfortable with the material coming through you. You can stop the channeling at any time.

In fact, when you learn to channel consciously, your sense of control may increase rather than decrease. That has been my experience. I can choose to focus on the outer world with my physical senses or to turn my attention inward to focus on more subtle inner experiences. I can choose which guide I tune into in much the same way I select a radio station. Demonstrating this kind of psychic flexibility has increased, rather than decreased, my sense of control.

Channeling has also strengthened my sense of control in another way. Because I have strong intuitive powers, in the past I have sometimes had a difficult time distinguishing my own feelings from the feelings I pick up from the people around me. I also used to have a tendency to lose myself in what others wanted me to be, neglecting my own needs and impulses. Channeling has greatly strengthened me in this area. When I channel, I have to ground and strengthen my own energy field before I can bring through the energy of another being. After I am fully grounded, I can experience the reality of another and my own reality simultaneously. The grounding and the simultaneous experiencing of realities have helped me to know my own boundaries and to recognize my own experience more clearly. This increased sense of my own boundaries has been one of the greatest benefits I have received from channeling.

The only warning I would give about channeling is that it might not be appropriate for you if you have a history of psychiatric disorders. For a moment, I would like to speak to you from the perspective I gained through my training in psychology.

As we have already discussed, channeling loosens

the control of your personality and allows you to experience different perspectives and different energies. For this reason, if you normally find it difficult to stay oriented in your life—if you have had frightening hallucinations, if you have had strong feelings of being persecuted, or have experienced strong mood swings—channeling might not be an appropriate avenue for you to explore.

If you are an average individual with a fairly well-organized life, with reasonably stable work and personal relationships, then channeling will expand your perspectives and options in an effective way. All of the channels I interviewed for this book pointed out ways in which the lessons and perspectives of their guides have enriched and stabilized their lives. However, accessing this particular kind of information requires you to move between different levels of consciousness and be capable of returning to a base of clear personality functioning. *If that personality base is severely impaired, you probably need to work on strengthening your personality, on strengthening your base of operations in the material world, before you move into other dimensions of experience.*

In general I find the relationship between mental illness and psychic phenomena an interesting one. Mental illness, from one perspective of modern medicine, occurs when the ego—the personality center of the individual—is overwhelmed by unconscious urges, often anger or sexual impulses. The ego, no longer able to mediate between these inner impulses and the world, ceases to maintain stability. In these cases the person may suffer from hallucinations, extreme mood swings, or delusions about the world.

You might have noticed a similarity here between what I have said about channeling and mental illness: both involve a loosening of the ego structure and a movement into altered states of consciousness. It is a well-known fact that people classified as mentally ill often exhibit an unusually high level of psychic abilities. This is no accident. When the habitual survival mechanisms of the personality are loosened, the person gains access to information and ways of knowing that the personality usually screens out. Unfortunately, this new psychic awareness is merged with painful psychological material; the conscious personality often becomes overwhelmed with a strange mishmash of accurate intuitive perceptions and distorted emotional responses. People who are mentally ill are immobilized by many aspects of psychic awareness. They have no ego controls and cannot move flexibly between the personality and intuitive states.

The mentally ill person stumbles onto intuitive states—including communication with spirit guides— through the disintegration of the controls of the personality, not through a conscious and systematic choice to move beyond the limitations of the personality. This person has no firm home base to return to. This disintegration of the home base is what propels the mentally ill into psychic experiences in the first place.

If you are a fairly stable person with no serious psychiatric history, you have a firm personality base. Your challenge will involve loosening the control of your personality system so that you can access subtle states of awareness. You need not worry about being overwhelmed, only about permitting yourself to open up sufficiently to allow the channeling experience to occur.

I believe that a new psychology has already begun to emerge. People trained in Western psychology have started to explore and write about the multidimensional mind. We no longer need to see ourselves as simply conscious personalities controlling painful unconscious material—we also have superconscious, multidimensional awarenesses. Unless we express a willingness to go beyond our personality, we will never experience these other dimensions. The truly evolved personality, no longer content to be limited to the rather restrictive perceptions of the personality, develops the ability to move flexibly between different states of awareness.

Doubt #3: *What If I Don't Like My Guide?*

You may be plagued with another doubt, closely

related to the fear of being overwhelmed: "What if I bring in a being that I don't like?"

If you follow the directions in this book, it is unlikely that you will ever attract a being that you don't like. However, if you do, just send the being away. It's as simple as that. This is one of the great advantages of conscious channeling: you meet your potential guide with all the resources and awareness with which you meet any human being.

Over the course of your life you have developed many skills that you use in assessing the character of those you meet. Some people do this intuitively and instinctively and call it "having gut feelings." Others make this assessment in a more logical fashion, analyzing the other person. Whatever particular strategy you use, you have picked up an important survival skill. As you begin to develop friendships with spirits, you will use these same skills.

In my own channeling experience I have only met one group of beings that I did not fully trust. Although I do not usually visualize my guides, I could see these beings clearly. The only extraterrestrial group that I have ever encountered, they were structurally similar to us, only smaller, and had large, slanted, yellow eyes.

I communicated with these guides for a three-month period. During this time they suggested that my partner Scott and I go to a certain spot in Arizona with cameras, and they wanted us to get there by a specific date and time. Due to various circumstances, we arrived a few days late. Although we could feel their presence very strongly on a telepathic level, we had missed the date for the sighting of their spacecraft.

During the time that we spent in Arizona, we channeled a lot of information from these beings. They claimed they were recruiting volunteers for a healing center where world leaders could come to experience extraterrestrial intelligence, and they wanted to know if we would participate. We had serious doubts, however. We felt that their timetable and their plan for development were pretty vague. And they did not seem overly concerned about how we would survive financially while working with them. This vagueness and insensitivity, in conjunction with the fact that we had never seen their spaceship, caused us to back away from the experience. We did not really have a bad experience with these extraterrestrials. It was actually rather interesting, but we intuitively knew that we didn't want to pursue the relationship. It taught us very clearly that discarnate beings have their own agendas and that we really need to tune into what they are to see how they fit with our own.

In teaching others how to channel, I have only met one student who drew to herself a guide that she didn't like. She promptly sent him on his way. Even in this case, I think that my student benefited from the encounter. She may have needed to demonstrate her own power to herself, since she has a difficult time saying no to her human friends. You might say that this spirit friend actually taught her an important lesson in self-assertion.

Although personally I have only met very loving beings and have only connected my clients with similar beings, I have heard a few stories, which may or may not be true. A few months ago, for example, I gave a talk on channeling. A man in his thirties, visibly upset, attended. When he asked to talk to me after the lecture, he confided that he was communicating with beings that had totally upset his life. He explained that dishes were breaking in his house and that he didn't know how to stop this disturbing phenomenon. Since I did not have the opportunity to talk to anyone else who had been in his home when these things happened, and since I had not seen them happen myself, I didn't know what to think. I couldn't determine if he was mentally ill, if he had actually had these very disturbing experiences, or if his situation had resulted from a combination of both factors. Since I had no accurate way to assess the situation, I decided to respond as if his story were true and to give him good practical advice on handling the situation. I suggested that he say a prayer for protection, that he visualize himself surrounded by a protective white light, and that he sit down in the presence of a friend and speak aloud to the being, making it clear that he did not want further contact. Finally, I suggested that he focus his attention away from the spirit world and ground his life in practical everyday ways. I recommended that if he continued to find himself drawn to the spiritual realms, that he direct that interest into a structured spiritual community which could offer him definite spiritual disciplines without encouraging his interest in psychic matters.

As I talked to this man, I could feel his resistance to what I was saying, and I confronted him with it. As we continued to talk, I could see that he was fascinated by the drama of this situation. Although he was scared, this kind of proof of other worlds had at the same time enthralled him. Clearly he wanted to draw me into the drama more than he wanted help in ending it.

As I mentioned earlier, I have no idea if this situation really occurred on an external level or not. It doesn't really matter. In either case, this man, intrigued by these kinds of manifestations, was drawing them to him. His fascination acted like a kind of magnet. I have no interest in dealing with those kinds of energies, so I literally don't attract them. The people I have taught to channel have been deeply interested in drawing highly evolved spirits who would never dream of violating their autonomy in any way. And they have uniformly attracted entities who met this description.

If you have relatively clear intentions and set healthy limits in your human relations, you should have no difficulty in drawing to you a highly evolved teaching guide. Just use your instincts, your good sense, and follow the instructions in Chapter Six on setting your intentions. To assist you in the process of assessing the quality of the guide you draw to yourself, I have included an etiquette chart of the behaviors you will and won't see in highly evolved guides.

HIGH GUIDES...	HIGH GUIDES DON'T...
* Respect your integrity and facilitate your own decision making	* Claim that they know what's best for you
* Humbly acknowledge a force greater than them	* Arrogantly claim that they are the ultimate source of wisdom and enlightenment
* Leave you feeling loved and inspired	* Leave you feeling powerless and dependent
* Say that many paths may lead to truth and expanded consciousness	* Say that there is only one path and that is their path
* Provide concisely stated information specific to your situation	* Speak in vague spiritual clichés that have little specific content
* Offer you counsel that challenges you and causes you to overcome personal limitations	* Flatter you and support you in negative emotional, mental, and physical patterns
* Serve those they can serve in a humble dedicated way	* Try to create a human following for themselves
* Have good manners, treat you respectfully, and contact you in times and places that are comfortable for you	* Have bad manners, intrude on you at awkward times, or abuse your body in any way

Releasing Your Doubts and Resistances

As you move closer toward learning to channel, be sensitive to any doubts that you experience. Allow them to arise. Don't suppress them. If you practice these exercises with a friend, discuss your doubts fully with her or him. If you do these exercises by yourself, you may want to write down your doubts and resistances as completely as possible. Then destroy the piece of paper. Burning it can serve as a particularly symbolic way to change the patterns of your doubts.

When we form any new relationship, anticipation and apprehension mingle, excitement and fear intertwine. Part of us longs for the new and part clings to the safety of the known. Allow yourself to experience both aspects of feeling as you move into this new kind of relationship. Enjoy both the anticipation and the trepidation that are an integral part of starting any new relationship.

Chapter Five

Preparing for Channeling

In reading the first chapters of this book, you may have wondered whether channeling is really accessible to everyone. You may have wondered whether some people might be more endowed with the talent of channeling than others.

The answers to these questions are paradoxical. Channeling is indeed a skill or function of consciousness that everyone possesses. However, it involves a level of openness and a level of receptivity that not everyone has yet developed. Some people do appear to demonstrate a greater facility in channeling than others, but in most cases these people have either worked very hard at developing more receptivity or they innately possess a high level of receptivity and openness.

People sometimes ask if prior development of psychic abilities is necessary in order to channel. People who have developed other psychic abilities such as clairvoyance (clear seeing) often possess the kinds of receptivity that allow channeling to occur, but these psychic abilities are *not* a prerequisite of channeling. The crucial factor here is psychic flexibility—the ability to move into an awareness different than that of the normal personality. And psychic flexibility does not depend on your ability to demonstrate other psychic abilities.

In this chapter we will look at how the personality

generally functions, and then look at different techniques that will allow you to relax the personality so
that you can develop the flexibility and receptivity
necessary for channeling.

The Structure of the Personality

Most metaphysical teachings share the understanding that the personality is made up of physical, emotional, and mental levels of functioning. On each of
these levels of experience we respond according to
certain habitual patterns. These three intimately connected levels form the personality, whose job it is to
promote our survival in the world.

The physical level of experience encompasses the
physical body and its characteristic ways of carrying
itself. Each of us develops a physical structure based on
the way we protect ourselves in the world. For instance, you may have noticed that some people walk
with their chests expanded and puffed out, while others walk with their shoulders hunched and their chests
imploded. These body postures indicate very different
ways of dealing with the world. The first person probably tries to make an impression through self-display.
The second most likely tries to efface himself and rein
in any emotional expression. Each of these stances indi-
cates the underlying survival strategy the individual employs. However, our physical structures do more than
just express underlying approaches to the world. These
postures also confine us, creating a limited and repetitive
experience of the world, because our bodies respond in
habitual ways to new stimulation and new experience.

In the same way, we all develop habitual patterns
of emotional response. We learn to see certain situations as dangerous to our needs and others as advanta-
geous, and we respond with habitual fear or joy or
anger in those situations. For instance, we have specific
experiences with our fathers and we see all men as
embodying the characteristics of our fathers. And just
as we learned to deal with our father in certain situations by conning or seducing or avoiding or lying, we

habitually act the same way with other men under similar circumstances. Each of us has developed our own intricate and subtle emotional response patterns as a means of surviving in life.

Finally, we all have mental patterns—particular beliefs and interpretations of the world based on our personal and cultural experience. We develop certain beliefs about how women should behave or about how men should behave, for example. We develop beliefs about what really motivates people, and then, based on the way we perceive them to be motivated, additional beliefs about how to get what we want from them.

Perhaps you saw a movie called *The Gods Must Be Crazy*. In it a Coke bottle is thrown from a plane and lands in a community of Kalahari bushmen in Africa. The bushmen, interpreting this bottle as a gift from the gods, proceed to use it in many innovative ways. Eventually possessiveness and violence develop in the community and one of the bushmen volunteers to walk the bottle to the edge of the world and throw it back to the gods.

The humor in this movie arises from the different realities that this single Coke bottle has. However, the movie has more to offer than just laughs. It provides a biting metaphor for the limited belief systems that all of us hold.

Thus, our personalities are made up of interlocking physical, emotional, and mental patterns. Our body takes on habitual stances based on the way we see and experience the world. Our emotions fall into patterned responses based on the way we see and interpret situations and on the way our body processes new input. Similarly, the patterns of our thought affect and are affected by our emotional and physical patterns.

Most of us are what spiritual teachers call asleep. We execute these physical, mental, and emotional patterns automatically and reflexively. Our perceptions and our consciousness are locked within the tight, interlocking circuitry of our bodies, emotions, and minds. If we find our particular patterns too painful, we may seek help from a specialist—a physical therapist or a

psychotherapist. Or we may mask these painful patterns with alcohol, drugs, eating, work, or sex. If these
masking responses become too extreme in themselves
(alcoholism, drug addiction, compulsive eating, over-
working, or sexual addictions), we may also turn to
specialists for help with our symptoms.

So what does this have to do with channeling?

The more individuals identify themselves with their
personalities, the more they cling to their own strate-
gies for survival, the less likely they are to develop
the flexibility and the openness needed to channel.
Conversely, the more you are able to achieve distance
from your personality and relax your habitual frame of
reference, the easier channeling will come to you.

Relaxing the Personality and Channeling

There are many ways to begin to loosen the hold
of our personalities on our consciousness, to break
away from our physical, emotional, and mental patterns of self-expression. As you learn to relax at these
different levels, to move away from your automatic or
habitual structures, you will begin to acquire the flexibility you need to experience new personal and new
transpersonal spiritual realities.

Throughout this chapter I will suggest specific
ways to relax your physical, emotional, and mental
patterns. Because these three spheres are all so closely
connected, working on any one of them will affect all of
the others, creating a greater flexibility in the personality in general. This chapter offers both long-term techniques for creating greater receptivity and openness
and more immediate techniques to use right before you
channel. Let yourself be drawn to the techniques that
feel right for you at a given time. Don't regard it as
compulsory to deal with all levels simultaneously.

Physical Relaxation

You can create greater openness in your physical
structure in many different ways. Passive methods of

physical relaxation involve being worked on by a skilled practitioner. These passive techniques include massage, deep-tissue work—rolfing, for example—which loosens habitual muscular patterns, or more traditional physical therapies that manipulate the body to facilitate healing. Some physical therapies also teach the body how to unlearn old patterns of movement and replace them with new, healthier patterns of movement. Rolf movement and traditional physical therapies are two of these. Conscious exercise programs, which involve selecting appropriate sports and exercises to eliminate the body's weaknesses, can also be used effectively. For instance, the character with the imploded chest mentioned in the last section might learn to lift weights, which will develop his pectorals and his lung capacity.

Perhaps the most balanced form of physical exercise is Hatha Yoga. A complete program of postures developed by yogis for the express purpose of releasing imbalances in the body, Hatha Yoga can help create a balanced, relaxed, and open body. Since the yogis developed these exercises specifically to prepare the body to carry expanded states of consciousness, Hatha Yoga is particularly relevant to our purposes here.

These long-term approaches will help break down physical defense structures and develop an open, flexible, and receptive body.

Now let's look at some physical exercises that you can use to relax just before you channel.

Proper Breathing
This is an important aspect of physical relaxation. Deep steady breathing can help dissipate a good deal of tension.

Breathing with Your Diaphragm
Stand, or sit comfortably in a straight-backed chair. Place your hands on the sides of your waist, fingers in front, thumbs in back. Lightly press in on your waist as you inhale deeply. As you breathe in, try to push your

hands away from each other using your diaphragm—the muscle that extends from just below your lungs to above your waist. The diaphragm should expand while inhaling and contract while exhaling. But your lungs will also expand as you inhale, pushing down on the diaphragm. You should be able to feel your diaphragm expanding near your waist.

Now exhale slowly, feeling the waist go in as your diaphragm and lungs contract. Slowly repeat this several times to help increase your awareness of the diaphragm, where proper breathing begins. You may find it relaxing during this exercise to imagine yourself inhaling a calming revitalizing energy and exhaling all your nervous tension.

Breathing Deeply

Close off your right nostril by pressing against it with one finger, and inhale deeply for a count of four. Then close off both nostrils and hold your breath for a count of twelve. Open your right nostril only and exhale slowly for a count of eight.

Now repeat this exercise. But this time close off the left nostril with one finger and inhale deeply for a count of four. Again close off both nostrils for a count of twelve, and opening your left nostril, exhale slowly for a count of eight.

Repeat this exercise five or six times, taking a slightly deeper breath with each cycle, until you work yourself to at least a count of six while inhaling. Each time concentrate on holding your breath three times as long as it took you to inhale; then take twice as long to exhale. By breathing more slowly and deeply, you will purge your body of tension.

Loosening Up

Stand straight and raise both arms as high as you can. Tighten every muscle in your body. Then lower your arms to your sides, relaxing your muscles as much as you can. Some muscles will probably still be tense, so it will help to repeat this exercise several times until you can feel every muscle relax.

As you perform this exercise, pay particular attention to your neck and shoulders. If you find extra tightness here, you might want to close your eyes and slowly rotate your head 90 degrees to the right and then 90 degrees to the left.

Relaxing the Body

Lie down on your back on a flat, comfortable surface. Starting with your feet, concentrate on relaxing each part of your body in turn. Imagine your feet becoming extremely relaxed. They feel heavier and heavier—almost as if they were made of lead. Repeat this image on every part of the body—moving slowly up your legs into your abdomen, through your torso, then up through your shoulders and neck to your head. When you complete this exercise, you will find yourself feeling completely relaxed and calm.

Emotional Relaxation

Just as physical habits prevent us from becoming as open and flexible as we can be, emotional habits and blockages also keep us from responding openly and receptively to life. As a long-term approach, many forms of psychotherapy can help release emotional blocks and patterns. Traditional verbal therapies such as psychoanalysis will help you become more aware of your emotional patterns—the ways in which you habitually respond, and the past origins of those responses. Verbal therapies, however, often do not allow for massive discharge of the anger and sadness that you may carry inside. Cathartic methods such as Gestalt therapy or Reichian therapy generally provide a good context for emotional release. Behavioral therapies such as Neurolinguistic Programming can help reprogram old emotional response patterns.

Each of these therapies offers a long-term strategy for working on emotional patterning. If, however, you need an immediate emotional relaxation technique—for example, if you approach a channeling session in emotional stress—here are some exercises that may help.

First, take some deep breaths. As you breathe in, imagine yourself inhaling peace and love. As you breathe out, imagine yourself exhaling the emotional situations that have produced your current stress. Repeat this for five or ten minutes.

Your breathing is linked to emotional stress as well as physical stress. When we are upset, we tend to take rapid, shallow breaths. Any of the breathing exercises detailed in the previous section will help to alleviate the physical patterns that accompany and reinforce emotional ·stress.

Taking a Color Bath

This exercise, which takes about ten to fifteen minutes, is extremely nurturing. Lie down on a flat, comfortable surface and breathe deeply. You might want to spend a minute or two just relaxing through deep breathing. Now visualize the color that you feel would be most healing to your present emotional state. You can choose any color. You will find that different colors have distinct appeals depending on your particular state. Just intuitively allow the healing color most appropriate to your emotions at this moment to come to you.

Now imagine that color as a small ball of light above your head. Slowly visualize that ball of light entering the crown of your head. See it filling your skull. Feel the light massaging your head and cleansing any tension from that part of your body. Now bring the light down into your throat. Be aware of any emotions that you wanted to express but didn't or that you have expressed but wish you hadn't. Allow your color to massage that area, cleaning out any tensions. Now move the light down through your shoulders into your chest cavity. Be aware of your heart. Acknowledge any hurts that you have suffered from others or have inflicted on others. Again let the light massage and soothe that area. Now move down to your solar plexus. Be aware of any tension you're carrying there. Recognize also any ways that you have used your power to harm others or have allowed others to exert power inappropriately over you. Again let your color massage, soothe, and cleanse that area. Now move your attention down to your abdomen. Be aware of any feelings of others that you have absorbed. Identify any sexual relationships that feel incomplete or any sexual tensions that you have. Again let the light cleanse and soothe those tensions. Finally move your attention down to the root of your spine. Let any feelings of fear about survival emerge, whether they involve money, work, or anything else. Let the color work with and wash away those fears. Now just let the light flow down from the top of your head through the different parts of your body it has already touched, down through your legs and feet. Imagine this flood of healing color coursing through you and eventually pouring into the earth. Glance up through your body. Do you feel any remaining tension or fear or anxiety? If you do, refocus the color and allow it to heal that area.

Mental Relaxation

Again, just as we have chronic physical and emotional patterns, we also acquire habitual mental patterns and beliefs. As a teacher of mine once said, "If you're a hammer, you see the world as a nail." We've all developed certain beliefs about the world—about who we are, about how other people operate, about how the world functions. At best these beliefs inhibit us from responding completely openly and receptively to life. At worst they create prisons of obsessive thinking, self-doubts, and paranoid delusions. Traditional verbal psychotherapies offer an excellent way of increasing our awareness of our hidden mental patterns.

If fearful self-doubting thoughts or excessive worry about something hinder your ability to relax, you will need to address this difficulty before you channel.

Rigorous exercise of any kind—jogging or biking, for example—will help. When your body reaches high levels of exertion, it secretes biochemicals called endorphins which create a sense of well-being and even elation. This state will act as an antidote to your negative thought patterns.

The color bath described in the last section will help create a sense of well-being that undercuts depressive thoughts.

Finally, any kind of willful meditation (see the next section) that involves concentrating on an external object will break the flow of your negative thinking by refocusing your attention.

Meditation, Spiritual Awareness, and Channeling

Now that we have addressed the physical, emotional, and mental aspects of our human experience—the parts of ourselves that comprise our personality—we need to turn to the spiritual level of our awareness.

The spiritual level is connected with experiences beyond our normal personality. Although we can use physical, emotional, and mental techniques to relax our personality structures, meditation is probably the most effective tool in preparing ourselves for expanded states of awareness. Meditation transports us to a state which is receptive to spiritual or nonphysical realities.

In the last twenty years a good deal of research has been done on the physiological aspects of meditation. Researchers have called meditation the fourth state of consciousness, because the corresponding physiological state differs from waking, sleeping, or dreaming. Oxygen consumption, carbon dioxide elimination, and the rate and volume of respiration decrease during meditation. The electroencephalograph, which measures brain waves, shows slow-moving alpha waves and occasional theta waves. Researchers often describe the state measured during meditation as one of wakeful relaxation.

Scientific research thus portrays meditation as a distinct state of consciousness. However, this research merely provides external corroboration of the inner experiences that yogis and other meditators have been having for years. Spiritual seekers have used meditation as a tool for thousands of years to move beyond the awareness of the personality into higher or more expanded states of awareness.

Although its primary function throughout history has been as a spiritual tool, meditation has also produced many beneficial side effects. Recognizing the deep relaxation that occurs during meditation, medical doctors have prescribed it for high blood pressure, migraines, and asthma. And recent studies have indicated that meditation can be very effective in addressing diseases of distress.

Meditators report feelings of serenity, tranquillity, and peacefulness during the early phases of meditation. Advanced meditators describe states of ecstasy, unconditional love, and union with all that is.

Because meditation relaxes the grasp that the personality has on consciousness, and opens one's awareness to inner realms of experience, this relaxation and openness carries over into the nonmeditative state. And as one begins to meditate over a long period of time, experiences of a psychic nature start to occur both during and outside of meditation. These psychic experiences may include clairvoyance, encounters with guides, telepathy, or psychic travels through the universe. From a yogic point of view these experiences are merely a side-effect of one's journey back toward one's true nature.

Yogis often view these experiences as nothing more than a distraction, and certainly not the goal of meditation.

I personally feel in alignment with most of these yogic ideas. As I see it, our common goal is to reunite with our essential multidimensional selves and to know our true relationship to the Great Self. However, I also recognize that meditation is a technique that some relationally oriented Westerners find difficult to comprehend. Working with spirit guides, a relational process, can help us to wake up to other aspects of our consciousness. We can use meditation to achieve our goal, or we can use our relationships with guides to do the same. But, because meditation is a tool for expanding consciousness, we can also use it to help us open to our spirit guides.

Techniques of Meditation

Let's look now at specific techniques of meditation that you might want to explore.

Although there are many different schools and methods of meditation, all willful techniques of meditation share this common thread: they still the mind, the working of the personality, by focusing on an object of meditation. This section presents two types of meditation—meditation through focusing on a visual object and meditation that uses sound. As you read through these descriptions, use your own instincts to determine which form suits you best.

Meditation is both an art and a science. And the stated goal of meditation, to still the mind—what we have called relaxing the personality—is much easier said than done. As you practice, you will find yourself distracted from the object of concentration by the chatter of your mind. Notice this happening, but then put it aside. Don't judge yourself harshly. Just gently bring your attention back to the object of your meditation. Even though you will probably be unable to still your mind immediately, the simple act of practicing meditation will break up the unchallenged dominance of your usual mental patterns and help loosen the hold of your thoughts.

Meditating Using Visual Imagination

Imagine a blank screen that hangs about six feet before your closed eyes. After you have created this screen in your mind, project onto it something simple and familiar—an orange or an apple, for example. Concentrate on making this object more and more real as you visualize it in three dimensions and in full color with all its details. Hold this object in front of your mind and think of nothing else. Once you have completely visualized your object, try to hold it in front of you for a minute without distraction. In subsequent meditations you can gradually extend the amount of time you spend holding this image without distraction.

Another way to meditate visually is to focus on an external object: a candle flame or a flower or a picture of someone you deeply respect. Again concentrate on this image without blinking, allowing no other thoughts

to interrupt your contemplation. In your first meditation, try to maintain your focus for two minutes.
Gradually increase your length of contemplation to ten
or fifteen minutes.

Meditating Using Sound as a Focus

Classical forms of meditation employ a mantra—a
sound repeated continually by the meditator to help
quiet the mind. Indian yogis have studied the affects of
different sounds on consciousness and have identified
certain sounds that can quiet the mind and bring us
into higher states of consciousness. These words, often
chosen from the Sanskrit language, may have associa-
tive meanings, but their real power lies in their vibrational frequency. *Om* and *Rama* are two commonly
used mantras.

If you know of a sound that you find intrinsically
attractive, feel free to use it. Although certain sounds
do have their own power, most of the power of a
mantra comes from the ability of the meditator to shut
off his or her usual mental processes.

Choosing Your Own Meditative Path

As you reread the exercises in this chapter, consid-
ering the techniques that will help prepare you for
channeling, realize that these same techniques will
increase not only your spiritual receptivity but your
general well-being. As you follow your own path toward an opening, trust your instincts in choosing the
technique most appropriate for you at any given
time. Feel free to change your technique whenever
you feel that you have truly completed an avenue of
relaxation. There are no rules that govern the spiritual path. No one else can define your path for unfolding.
Trust your intuition, and enjoy the process of learning
and expanding your levels of relaxation and receptivity.

A Developmental Model for Channeling

As you prepare to channel, you might find it
helpful to look at a model of the developmental stages

of channeling. Perhaps it can serve as a map for you, increasing your understanding of the journey you are about to embark on.

This model was developed by Dr. Margo Chandley of Beverly Hills, California. Dr. Chandley, a researcher, recently completed a four-and-a-half-year study of thirteen mediums (channels). From her research, Dr. Chandley defined channeling as the process of learning to bring nonphysical spiritual energies into the physical realm. She observed seven stages of development that channels go through from the time they first have nonphysical experiences—such as out-of-body experiences or hearing inner voices—to the time when they have fully integrated this level of reality into their normal personalities. In a recent interview, Dr. Chandley told me:

> I feel that the whole channeling process is about connecting to another dimensional reality that we haven't yet been able to prove scientifically. I base my feelings on my own study with channels, some of whom had been channeling for fifteen years. In the four-and-a-half-year process of the study, I watched the evolution of their consciousness, what they went through. Changes in their total personality became part of the channeling process and part of their personal challenge.
>
> What they all seemed to come to toward the end of the study was that this is a way of becoming spirit in the physical. They all seemed to feel that we are becoming part of a nonphysical reality, that we are no longer just physical beings on a planet but that we are becoming unified with spirit.

The seven-step process, described by Dr. Chandley in *A Psychological Investigation of the Development of the Mediumistic Process in Personality Function*, proceeds in the following manner:

Phase One—Conceptualization

In this phase the channel remembers an experience of nonphysical reality. This experience could involve hearing voices, seeing apparitions, having an out-of-body experience, or having unusual experiences of energy.

Phase Two—Preparation

In this stage the individual prepares to accept nonphysical energies through processes such as deep relaxation, meditation, and visualization.

All of the channels interviewed in Chapter Two spoke of going through this kind of preparatory stage. They either consciously attempted to learn how to channel or they learned how to channel after several years of pursuing their own growth through meditation and other processes. The material included in this chapter also falls under the second phase of Chandley's schema. If you have been practicing relaxation and meditative techniques for a while, you are well into your preparatory phase. If you have just begun to pursue your growth in this way, you are at the beginning of the preparatory phase.

Phase Three—Gestation

In this stage the channels begin to feel distinctly physical and nonphysical energies within themselves. Physical discomfort—between the shoulder blades, in the solar plexus, in the head and neck, in the spinal column—may accompany this stage as the physical body adjusts to nonphysical energies.

None of the channels I interviewed spoke of experiencing physical discomfort. I, too, have never experienced discomfort, and neither have most of my students. However, a few of my students have told me of feeling pressure in different parts of their bodies as they brought in new energies.

Phase Four—Recognition

At this stage the channel moves forward in defining a relationship to the nonphysical energy system, an identification that often includes giving a name to the nonphysical energy system. This phase often marks a turning point in that the channel may move backward into Phase Three for further gestation or may move forward into verbal channeling.

Phase Five—Activation

In this phase the channel makes a conscious choice to become a verbal channel. By bringing the nonphysical energy system into alignment with their physical energy system, channels are now able to transmit the wisdom and information they receive in verbal form.

Phase Six—Integration

At this point trust has developed between the physical and the nonphysical energy systems. The channel radiates comfort and trust in the process. Now, the channel may make a living from an activity related to channeling such as counseling, consulting, or professional channeling.

Phase Seven—Maturation

In this phase a new question arises: Does a separate mediumistic personality still exist, or have the first six phases led to a final self-actualized personality in whom physical and nonphysical energies are integrated into one unit, one aware personality? At this point the level of integration between the two systems is so high that the separate nonphysical entity may disappear.

A Final Word

As you prepare yourself for channeling by using the relaxation techniques in this chapter and your own techniques, you are following a course of development that many channels have followed before. However, because you have approached the development of this skill consciously, you have the good fortune to be aware of the process as you enter it, and to have the opportunity to chart your own progress as you develop. This distinguishes you from the channels who began their work a generation ago. With fewer forerunners charting the way for them, these channels often doubted their own sanity as they went through the different phases of their development.

Enjoy each phase. As many sages have said, the importance of the endpoint pales in comparison to the experience of the present moment. The process of awakening to our essential multidimensional natures is the hallmark of human existence. Enjoy your development as a channel as part of that process.

Chapter Six

Invoking Your Personal Spirit Guides

If you have practiced the techniques offered in Chapter Five, and have increased your level of relaxation and your receptivity to channeling, then you are now ready to begin building your relationship with your guide.

Several types of relationships with spirit guides are possible. The relationship may already be established; if so, you will only need to tune in to what is already there. Spirit guides who love us and watch over us exist, regardless of whether we are aware of them or not. We all have members of our soul group and parts of our own multidimensional self (See Chapter Three) available to us. And each of us can turn to a higher self for support and guidance.

We may also have made pre-incarnational agreements with entities quite different from us. Both Sanaya Roman and Darryl Anka mentioned that they had pre-incarnational work agreements with their guides. In this kind of contractual situation, the process of contacting guides is like remembering a long-forgotten promise.

Finally, we may consciously set out to form new relationships by attracting new guides to teach us special skills or specialized knowledge. These guides, who come from many different dimensions of experience, can have widely varying specialties.

With so many guides already available to us, and the potential to attract many more, we need to make some important choices. As you move toward forming a relationship with a guide, it is important that you envision more clearly the kind of guide you want to work with, and the kind of relationship. By defining the relationship, you will ensure that you initially begin working with the guide best suited to your current needs and desires. By clarifying and defining your intentions, you will also begin to see yourself as a powerful participant in this new kind of relationship. You will plainly know the kind of experience you hope to share with a guide, and you will establish a baseline that will allow you to assess whether the relationship that develops meets your expectations.

Sometimes people go into channeling mistakenly believing that "guides know best." In fact, you are always the best expert on yourself. You are always the one who knows your *own* deepest truth in any situation.

Guides can increase your understanding and challenge the beliefs that limit you in your life. They can offer you comfort and counsel in difficult situations. They can open you to your own higher intuitional capacities and help you see your own multidimensional nature. *But ultimately you must decide if your guide's perspectives and advice apply to your unique situation. Guides provide many things, but in the final analysis, the responsibility for your destiny rests entirely in your own hands.* For this reason, it is essential to begin channeling with a firm sense of your own goals and intentions, and a sense of yourself as a powerful cocreator of the relationship.

As a final word, let me note that guides and human beings are not matched according to type. You need not look for any particular *type* of guide based on your perceptions of who you are. Rather, as you clarify your intentions and needs, you will create a magnetic pull that will attract the guide most appropriate to you at this time.

Creating an Invocation for Your Guide

Sit down with a piece of paper and pencil close at hand. Make sure you feel comfortable and relaxed. Take a few deep breaths. Pay attention to your belly as you inhale and exhale. As you inhale, your belly should expand; as you exhale, your belly should contract. When you pay attention to your breathing in this way, you may feel a warmth or tingling in your belly. Enjoy these sensations and take a few more deep breaths.

Now you are ready to begin clarifying your intentions, paying particular attention to three specific questions:

1. What do you want to learn from your guides?
2. What qualities do you desire in a guide?
3. What kind of relationship would you like to have with your guide?

1. Clarifying What You Want to Learn

Let's start with what you want to learn from your guide. Make a list. Be honest. Don't limit yourself to goals that you regard as noble or spiritual. Anything you really want to learn from a guide is fair game. Here are some examples:

> I would like to learn how to become more successful in my work.
> I would like to learn to express myself more spontaneously and freely.
> I would like to develop my healing abilities.
> I would like to learn to be more assertive.
> I would like to learn to get along better with my children.
> I would like to learn to have out-of-body experiences.

Continue adding goals to your list until nothing else comes to mind. Don't limit yourself to any set number of goals. I have seen lists with just three or four, and I have seen lists three pages long. The simple act of clarifying your current ambitions help attract a guide capable of working toward them. This goal setting will also orient you to the idea of receiving spirit guidance in the important matters of your life.

2. Clarifying Qualities You Desire in a Guide

Now that you've listed the things you wish to learn, let's look at the qualities you would like your guides to have. In many ways guides are like people. Each has a distinct personality. Some are humorous; others serious. Some are highly intellectual; others shy away from intellectualizing. Some are disciplined and methodical; others playful and whimsical. Some are patient; others impatient. Some are humble; others arrogant. So consider carefully the personal qualities you would like your guide to have. A relationship with a guide is just as intimate as a relationship with a lover or close friend. You want to choose prudently the kind of being with whom you will share this close experience.

Again take a few breaths. Close your eyes and reflect on this question. When you feel ready, begin to write down the qualities you would like to see in your guide. Some examples follow:

> I want my guide to be humorous and playful.
> I want my guide to be honest with me—to praise my strengths and point out my weaknesses.
> I want my guide to be wise and to understand spiritual matters.
> I want my guide to be patient and caring.
> I want my guide to know about medicine and healing.
> I want my guide to be loving and kind.

You might want to give some thought to the question of whether it matters to you if your guide is on the human chain of evolution or not.

Many wise guides have never incarnated in a physical body. They do not necessarily understand what it is like to inhabit a human body. Since they may not share our view of time and space, they may find it difficult to understand our feelings of frustration and impatience as we create our lives in linear time. On the other hand, guides who have never lived on Earth can offer us fascinating pictures of life in other parts of the universe. Through contrast, they can also give us new perspectives on our earthly lives. For instance, Bashar, Darryl Anka's guide, claims that animals on Essassani are nonterritorial. This simple idea provides an intriguing contrast to animal and human behavior on our planet, opening up an alternative vision of a nonterritorial world.

As you set your intentions, you might find that you want to experience many different kinds of guides. You may feel reluctant to choose just one of many contradictory desires. Ultimately you need not limit yourself to one guide, anymore than you have to limit yourself to one human friend. Just as you make different human friends who reflect various aspects of your interests, so you can create relationships with guides whose individual qualities and areas of specialization differ.

Currently I am working with Walter, a guide who excels at conscious decision making. Through visualization of the probable outcomes of various decisions, he leads me to make the best choice. I also work very closely with the Sisterhood, a group of feminine beings, from both our planet and other worlds, who teach feminine spiritual wisdom. I also channel my own expanded awareness, my higher self.

As you open the gates to the unseen realms, you have the potential to meet many spirit friends who will share with you in different ways. Sometimes new guides will present themselves to you while you are trying to contact old ones, and sometimes you may initiate contact with new guides by praying for help or creating a new invocation. Spirit friends tend to come and go in our lives; they vary in their importance to us at different times, just as our human friends do.

For now, however, concentrate on creating the one

relationship that seems most fitting to you given your list of qualities. Your success in building this first relationship will stimulate you to seek other spirit friends and vice versa.

3. Clarifying the Relationship You Want with Your Guide

Now let's focus on the kind of relationship you want to have with your guide. At first glance this might seem identical to the issue we just addressed. However, although the two questions are similar, they do differ in one significant respect. In the previous list, you concentrated on the qualities you want your spirit guide to possess. In this list you will focus on the relationship itself. Here are some examples:

> I want to have a relationship with my guide that is mutually rewarding. I want both of us to learn and benefit from it.
> I want a relationship with my guide where there is complete honesty.
> I want my relationship with my guide to be primarily verbal. I want us to be able to discuss different things together.
> I want my guide to be more of a peer than a mentor.
> I want a relationship with a guide that stimulates me but also feels safe and secure.
> I want to have fun with my guide.

Writing Your Invocation

Now that you have created three separate lists of hopes and intentions, it is time to fashion them into an invitation to your spirit friends.

First decide how you would like to refer to your guide. Do you want to call him or her a spirit guide? A teacher? A spirit friend or companion? Once you have selected a term, start a new piece of paper with the words, "I am calling to myself a spirit guide (or whatever term you have chosen) who . . ." Then begin to list under this invocation the qualities you have written down during this exercise.

An example of an invocation to a guide follows:

I am calling to myself a spirit friend who . . .
    can teach me greater self-knowledge and help me express myself more freely
    can teach me to communicate more clearly with others
    can help me be more assertive with others, especially members of my family
    can help me develop patience, particularly with my children
    can help me find my own creative direction
I am calling to myself a spirit friend who is
    intelligent
    wise and compassionate
    funny
    patient
    has been a parent
    has lived on earth
    understands and likes me
I am calling to myself a relationship with a spirit friend that
    nurtures and supports me
    is mutually honest
    is gentle and nondemanding
    is something I can depend on in my life

When your invocation feels complete, sign and date it. Then say it aloud three times. Because you are extending an invitation to a new friend, you will want to say it with attention and love.

In Chapter One I referred to the law of vibrational attraction. As you repeat your invocation aloud, you will be putting your request into sound vibrations and sending your vibration into the universe, where it will invariably attract beings of compatible vibration.

Repeat this exercise, saying your invocation aloud three times every day for at least five days. You do not need to set a specific time or place, just find a convenient time at some point during each of the next five days. Repeating this exercise will help maintain your focus on attracting this kind of relationship. And repetition will also increase the effectiveness of your request. You will be like a radio tower, sending out your signal and waiting for a response to come. At this point you need not try to decipher any response. Simply be aware that you have sent out a signal; a response will certainly come.

Chapter Seven

How to Channel

In practicing the relaxation exercises in Chapter Five, and in creating your personal invocation according to the method outlined in Chapter Six, you have systematically prepared yourself for channeling. You have already practiced creating the open, relaxed state necessary for channeling, and you have clarified your intentions and sent out an invitation to an appropriate guide. Now you are ready to become a vessel or receiver for the energy and wisdom of your spirit guide.

My first guide, Diya, originally taught me the channeling method I will share with you here. It is an effective and fun technique which my students have enjoyed learning.

Grounding and the Energy Body

In the metaphysical understanding of the world, we as beings house a subtle energy body. This energy body has its own network of energy channels that parallel the arteries and veins of the physical body. The subtle energy body is equipped with its own senses, which parallel the five physical senses. Whenever we channel or demonstrate other psychic abilities, our subtle energy body resonates to the energy body of another. We receive impressions of the other being through these inner senses.

Effective psychic work or channeling always demands that we create a conscious, stable connection between the physical body and the subtle body. Only then can we receive impressions from a spiritual entity. The technique that creates the stabilization necessary to make this connection is called grounding. Grounding connects the channel with the earth, allowing the energy body to vibrate at the higher level of energy required to resonate to our guides, yet at the same time permitting us to remain calm and centered in ourselves.

The vase technique you will learn is a particular method of grounding that will encourage you to become a conduit or vessel for the energy of another being. It will provide you with the stability you need to resonate to your guides while remaining firm and centered in your own physical experience.

As I pointed out in Chapter One, channeling and trance go hand in hand. Trance creates a deeply relaxed state that makes it possible to release your normal personality and resonate deeply with another. The vase technique allows you to enter a light trance and resonate deeply to your guide while maintaining a sense of your own boundaries.

Have fun with this exercise. Enjoy it as an experience in its own right, apart from its facilitation of channeling. This exercise works best if you have a partner who can read the instructions to you. If you do not have a partner, read the instructions into a tape and play it back to yourself when you want to try the exercise. Only if you have no other alternative, read the instructions to yourself, then close your eyes and follow them from memory. This, the least desirable approach, has the disadvantage of distracting your full attention from the internal focus channeling demands.

If you decide to make a tape, speak slowly and deliberately, leaving a minute after each instruction so that as you channel, you will have a chance to respond aloud to each question. If a partner guides you through this technique, remind him or her to pause after each instruction, giving you all the time you need to respond aloud. To prevent any gaps or authorial asides from distracting you from the exercise, all directions have been italicized. Instruct your partner (or in making a tape remember) to read only these italicized words aloud.

Imagining Your Vase

To practice the vase technique, first relax using any of the suggestions in Chapter Five of this book or any of your own favorite methods. As soon as you have completed your preliminary relaxation exercises, *close your eyes and pay attention to your breathing. Feel the weight of gravity pulling on your body. Feel the weight of your limbs and torso as you sit. Pay special attention to your belly as you inhale and exhale. Watch the expansion of your belly as you inhale and the contraction of your belly as you exhale. Spend at least five minutes relaxing and paying attention to your breath.*

Now slowly begin to imagine a vase approximately three feet in front of you.

Notice the colors of the vase.

Notice its texture. Is there a pattern on the outside? Is there a difference between the texture on the inside and the outside of the vase?

Notice the shape of the vase. How tall is it? What does the mouth of the vase look like?

Notice the weight of the vase.

Notice the strength and sturdiness of the vase. Is the vase secure and stable? If not, give it a stand or reproportion it so that it sits securely on the earth.

Here is an example.

> *Instruction:* Notice the colors of the vase.
> *Response:* It's an almost translucent blue with streaks of pink and silver running through it.
> *Instruction:* Notice its texture. Is there a pattern on the outside? Is there a difference between the texture on the inside and the outside of the vase?
> *Response:* No, no distinct pattern. Streaks of silver and pink flowing in delicate steamers

through the blue glass. It's beautiful. The inside and the outside are the same. Light shines through it.

If you answer these questions from memory, simply keep a general sense of them in your mind and begin to describe the vase aloud as thoroughly as you can.

As you explore your vase, enjoy its beauty. Indulge all of your senses in viewing it. When you feel that you know your vase well, slowly bring it closer to your body. Bring it closer and closer until you merge with it.

As you merge with the vase, feel fully what it is like to be that vase. Now, using the first person singular pronoun, slowly begin to describe yourself aloud.

For instance:

I am the vase. I am made of blue glass streaked with pink and silver streamers. I am translucent. Light shines through me. I am fairly new. I look delicate but I'm actually quite strong. I have a stable, rounded bottom that sits securely on a table. I narrow at the neck and have a fluted mouth. I am beautiful to look at. I love to be filled with wild flowers and lilies.

Take approximately ten minutes to *feel yourself as the vase. Feel the empty space you enclose. Feel your openness and your willingness to be filled. Also feel the solidity of your walls. Feel yourself as the strong boundaries that enclose the space.*

As the vase you have both firm external boundaries and an inner openness. Feel both simultaneously. Practice moving back and forth between being the solid boundaries and the open receptivity. Identifying simultaneously with your own solidity and your own receptivity is the dual perception of conscious channeling.

Enjoying Your Vase

Most of my students have enjoyed exploring their vases. People tend to choose vases that they find deeply healing in some way. The colors chosen, the womblike nature of the vase, and its beauty all combine to create healing sensations of satisfaction and comfort.

I have taken pleasure in learning the variety and beauty of my students' vases. One student created a jade vase decorated with elephants. Another formed an ancient, iron-red water vessel with barely visible markings on it. Another student chose a beautiful crystal vase, setting it on a tripod of gold lion's feet decorated with jewels and gilded flowers. Another saw a vase of unearthly blue which stimulated feelings of peace and serenity in him.

Perhaps the most interesting vase described to me was one visualized by a psychotherapist. He imagined his vase as a cylinder with Egyptian profiles on it. However, this was no ordinary vase. It emitted sounds and colors from his first contact with it. It soon became clear that this vase did not merely serve as a tool for grounding, it was a complex source of information in itself. In time this man learned to visualize himself walking around inside the vase as if it were a library, and to see himself picking out volumes of information on any topic. He could choose volumes that covered any subject at any period of time. Once he had selected a volume, the information contained inside appeared to him through images, sounds, and emotions.

I, too, have had deeply satisfying meditative experiences while exploring my vase. I have felt myself filled with great serenity and waves of blissful feelings. So enjoy this part of the teaching; it has many inherent pleasures connected with it.

Integration and Practice with Your Vase

Now that you have learned to merge with your vase, you can integrate all that you have practiced so far and prepare yourself in earnest for channeling. *For the next five days, set aside half an hour a day to practice.* You need not choose the same time each day. If you miss a day, just pick up on the following day where you left off. Follow each of these four steps every day.

Step One

Perform the relaxation exercises you have chosen from Chapter Five or your own preferred relaxation exercises. Spend ten to fifteen minutes just relaxing.

Step Two

Read your invocation aloud three times to declare your intention to call your guide to yourself.

Step Three

Close your eyes and visualize your vase. Merge with it. Feel yourself as both the solid walls of the vase and the waiting emptiness inside.

Step Four

Recall your intention to connect with your guide, and see if you can sense any presence around you as you sit merged with your vase.

Receiving Information from Your Guides

You can receive information and make contact with your guides in many different ways. Your guides exist in inner dimensions or planes that are inaccessible to your physical senses. As you begin to open yourself to your guides, you will develop the senses you need in order to make the contact. The inner senses you will discover include sight, hearing, smell, touch, and taste. In addition, an inner kinesthetic sense allows us to feel empathic sensations in our body. For instance, if you resonate to someone with a lung disease, you may feel pain in your lungs. Or if you resonate to someone in a state of meditative bliss, you may feel your heart expanding as blissful feelings enter your own heart. A final inner sense is one of pure knowing—unconnected with any particular sensory experience.

Most individuals rely on one predominant inner sense that they use to receive information from subtle dimensions. They seldom depend on the "secondary" senses in acquiring channeled information. For instance, my primary inner sense is hearing. I hear my guides, I feel their energy resonating with mine, and I experience an inner knowing about much of what they say to me. I very rarely receive visual or tactile information.

In contrast, one of my best friends receives primarily visual information. When she brings a question to her guides, she initially feels their presence and then often perceives a visual image or witnesses a dreamlike sequence. She may spend weeks trying to decipher the meaning of this symbol and its applicability to her question. Unraveling the meaning of these symbols plays an important part in her growth process. As she makes associations between the symbol and the circumstances of her own life, stories and further images come to her that carry information about her life and the lives of her clients or the people close to her. She and I look at each other with mutual envy and appreciation. I sometimes wish that my guides would offer me more visual intelligence, and she occasionally wishes that she could receive information as clearly defined as mine. The real point I want to make is that there is no better or worse way. We all receive information through the interplay of our inner senses with our personality in our own unique way.

Sitting with Your Vase

As you sit merged with your vase, simply notice what happens. *Don't try to force anything to happen.* Don't try to initiate verbal communication. Just pay attention to what happens after you have set your intentions, grounded yourself, and turned inward for a response.

Although everyone's first contact with the inner worlds is unique, you can anticipate experiencing one of the following.

1. Initially nothing may happen. You may sit merged with your vase, feeling totally bored. You may feel a little foolish and decide to treat this book to an early retirement. If this happens, just try to remain relaxed

and calm. Remain merged with your vase and continue to observe what happens.

2. You may begin to feel unusual sensations of energy in different areas of your body. Certain parts (a hand, your throat, a foot, your spine) may begin to tingle or vibrate. Stay relaxed and calm. Remain merged with your vase and observe what happens.

3. Your body may move in unusual patterns. You may feel energy coursing through you. You may alter your breathing. You may find your mouth puckering or your posture shifting. Stay relaxed and calm. Remain merged with your vase and observe what happens.

4. Unusual images may appear in your mind's eye. You may see a figure whom you assume to be your guide. You may catch sight of little creatures that are unfamiliar to you. Images may remain stable or they may move erratically. Stay relaxed and calm. Remain merged with your vase and observe what happens.

5. You may feel a subtle presence in front of you, beside you, or behind you. Stay relaxed and calm. Remain merged with your vase and observe what happens.

6. You may experience shifts in temperature. You may feel uncomfortably hot or uncomfortably cold. Stay relaxed and calm. Remain merged with your vase and notice what happens.

Again, *there is no right or wrong way.* There is only one way to make contact with your guide, and that is *your* way.

Making Direct Contact with Your Spirit Guide

After you have spent several days practicing the vase technique and alertly noting any responses from your guide, you can attempt to make direct contact. Hopefully both you and your guide have enjoyed the flirtation. Now it is time to initiate a direct dialogue with your guide.

Prepare for this contact in the usual manner. Perform your relaxation exercises, say your invocation aloud three times, and merge with your vase. This time, however, instead of just sitting and observing, begin to establish direct contact. Dialogue with a guide is much the same as dialogue with any other being. Follow your natural curiosity in posing questions, and then wait for the answers to come. You might want to ask one or more of the following: "Is anyone there?" "Do you have a name?" "What world do you live in?" "How are you connected with me?" After this initial contact, feel free to ask any questions on which you would like your guide's perspective.

You can ask these questions either aloud or internally. You will find it helpful to have an idea of what you want to ask before you actually sit down to channel. Once you are grounded in the vase, you have entered a light trance state, which makes the rational part of your mind, the part that asks questions, less accessible. So devote a little time to thinking about what you want to ask before you begin. Even better, if you work with a partner or have an interested friend, ask that person to pose the questions for you once you feel you have connected with your guide. You can give your friend a written list beforehand or just orally enumerate the questions you'd like him or her to ask.

Even if the perspective seems alien to you, try to remain open to the material you receive. The first sentence I ever channeled, as I mentioned earlier, was, "We would like to assure you that angels do exist." This statement startled me because I didn't really believe that guides existed and I certainly didn't believe in angels.

One of my clients contacted a discarnate entity who is a Taoist yogi. This guide first entered doing somersaults and cartwheels in front of my client. Needless to say, this was nothing like the dignified entrance that my client had expected from a spiritual teacher. It provided, however, an accurate preview of the humor and unpredictability this guide would use to challenge my client's habitual ways of perceiving. My client showed great mental flexibility in allowing himself to accept this information. And that's the point. We turn to discarnate teachers because we want to enlarge our perspective. But to allow this enlargement, we have to remain receptive to input that may challenge our ordinary perspectives.

As you have gathered by this time, visual or kinesthetic information is at least as important and valuable as verbal communication. However, most of us in this culture have a bias toward words. We feel that if we can call something by its name, we will have a deeper understanding of it. If you would like to establish verbal communication with your guide but are having difficulty, you may want to try the following exercise.

Step One

Do your relaxation exercises.

Step Two

Say your invocation to your guide.

Step Three

Visualize your vase and merge with it.

Step Four

Pretend that you are your guide. Speak to yourself aloud as if you were sitting a few feet away. Begin to offer yourself guidance on the topic you want to address. Listen inside for the guidance to give yourself and then begin to speak aloud. Refer to yourself in the second person. For instance, "You feel nervous about our current interaction. You are afraid you are making it up."

You may feel some embarrassment while performing this exercise. But though it may feel silly, this exercise is one of the best ways I know to open up the verbal channel between you and your guide.

Establishing Nonverbal Contact

Sometimes the relationship between a guide and a channel is primarily nonverbal. I once had a student who very rarely received verbal information. Rather, his guide would come to him through visual imagery. Fascinating inner movies would unfold in which my student's guide would appear to him in humorous costumes or take him through different scenes on horseback or just tell him to sit down and relax. In approaching my student, the guide employed surprise, humor, and the ability to create relaxing situations for him to experience. The guide seemed determined to upset any of my student's preconceived notions, to do the opposite of what the channel expected. He consistently offered this message: "Lighten up and enjoy yourself. Don't take yourself so seriously." As a psychotherapist, I could see that this man was somewhat rigid emotionally and mentally. And although he felt frustrated by the lack of verbal communication, I regarded his guide's approach as the perfect way to help him develop.

Other people, instead of establishing verbal contact with their guides, see colors or feel a healing presence. I have a friend whose guides come to her in the form of colors and kinesthetic sensations of angelic presences. However, when she asks for verbal teachings, her guides always tell her, "Pay attention to the everyday details of your life and learn from them." Since my friend has highly attuned psychic abilities, but has difficulty focusing on the more practical aspects of her life, her guides' approach seems very sensible to me.

You may prefer verbal communication but only experience nonverbal guides. Or conversely, you may prefer nonverbal communication and meet only verbal entities. In either case, try to remain open and receptive to whatever form your guidance and healing comes in. Whether you realize it or not, you have your own natural way of opening to other states of awareness. The more you encourage the experiences that come naturally, the more they will take the form that is right for you.

Although most of the people I have taught to channel have learned to channel verbally, some have learned to draw comfort and a sense of engagement from their guides without the exchange of words. If you keep knocking at the door of the unseen, the being or energy most appropriate to you will eventually open the door.

A final word. You may find yourself feeling tired as you begin to channel. This quite normal reaction offers an excellent sign that you are really channeling. It takes time for the body to build up its tolerance. When I first began to contact spirit guides, I could only channel for ten minutes at a stretch. I have now built up a kind of endurance and can channel for fifty or sixty minutes without stopping. Even now, however, toward the end of that hour, I still become tired. Recognize and honor your own limits: stop channeling when it becomes too draining for you. The process of building psychic stamina is the equivalent of building physical endurance in any sport.

As you learn to channel, enjoy yourself. Allow the method that seems most natural to you to unfold. Trust your own method of channeling. And finally, take good care of yourself. If you become tired or experience any kind of discomfort, stop channeling. Whether your contact is verbal or nonverbal, you should come away from it feeling uplifted and nurtured.

Chapter Eight

Building a Relationship with Your Guide

Building a relationship with your guide is similar to establishing any relationship: the quality depends on the time and care you put into it. In channeled relationships, however, unique challenges arise based on the fact that you live in a body and your guide does not. The most fundamental challenge that you will need to meet is doubt. You do not doubt that your mother or lover or boss exists. At times these people are all too real. But doubts about whether your guide really exists or not may nag at you, undermining your efforts to build this kind of relationship. In addition, society sanctions most earthly relationships that you form. Your friends may not like your mother or boss but they will never question the acceptability of these kinds of relationships. However, you may receive only minimal social support in maintaining a relationship with your guides.

In my experience three distinct but closely related avenues of approach will allow you to build a rich, healthy relationship with your guide:

1. addressing your doubts
2. committing time to channeling
3. building a support system

Addressing Your Doubts

The most common and paralyzing doubt that people encounter is connected with the subtle nature of channeling. As people begin to channel, they almost inevitably feel as if they are making it up. The greatest channels of this century, Edgar Cayce and Jane Roberts, went to their graves with doubts about the origin of the material they channeled. Like most channels, I am my own greatest doubter. I constantly compare my conscious viewpoint with that of the material I channel, to see if I can pinpoint a difference in perspective. I analyze channeled material carefully, looking for any signs that it might actually be repressed responses that I could not allow into consciousness any other way. Self-doubt is part of channeling. When you feel as if you are making it up, you have tapped into one of the occupational hazards of channeling.

We raise these questions for a number of reasons. For one, the inner senses and the inner planes of experience are so much more subtle than the outer planes and the physical senses. To make the transition between these planes even more difficult, we have been raised in a culture that doesn't acknowledge or respect this difference. As I noted earlier, scientific thinking invalidates the inner worlds. When you begin to approach your guides, you will need to challenge much of your cultural conditioning. It takes a lot of motivation and discipline to accept this challenge.

The fact that channeled information filters through your own thinking and language patterns only compounds the doubt of making it up. Channeling always involves the resonance of two energy systems: those of the guide and the channel. But we translate this experience of resonance into our own concepts and words. Channeled messages therefore come through using our own vocabulary and metaphors.

For instance, your guide may want to encourage you to be patient with your own growth process. If you were a gardener, you would be used to nurturing your plants and waiting patiently for them to bear fruit in their own time. You may translate your guide's insight into an analogy between the natural growth cycles of plants and your own growth process. Yet when you examine the channeled material, you may have difficulty believing that this channeling represents anything more than your own mind at work. After all, the plant imagery arose from your own personal experience.

Ultimately we can never know for sure whether channeling is a fabrication of our own minds, a relatively unexplored mind function, or true communication with other beings. We have no systematic way to resolve this question. But the way I look at it, if we have invented all these channelings, then the human mind has an amazing capacity to access wisdom far beyond our conscious knowledge. And if we have not made it up, then the universe is full of many wise beings who love us and want to help us. Pick your miracle. Either alternative should excite and enliven you.

Instead of judging the "reality" of channeling, take a look at the bottom line. Does the channeled material help you and others? Does it enrich your life? Does it offer you anything of value? If it doesn't, then why continue, regardless of whether channeling is part of your own mind or actual communication with another being? But if it does help you, then why stop just because you can't know for certain where it comes from?

When my students complain that they're just making it up, I tell them, "Good. Continue to make it up." Allow your imagination to roam freely. The rational mind judges whether something is valid in terms of the physical senses and the outer world. Honor the rational mind: it has a valued place in securing your survival. But if you want to do intuitive work, if you want to explore the inner worlds and your relationship with guides, you must temporarily allow your intuitive mind and the inner senses to rule. When you try to channel, you may hear your rational mind saying, "Am I making it up?" But don't allow the rational mind to rule during that time. Push its thoughts aside; soon enough it will be back in control.

You may find these suggestions helpful in dealing with your doubts about the origin of channeled material.

1. Record your channeled sessions and play them back later.

When I first began to channel, I taped every session and played it back several times. When I replayed these sessions, I listened to the different speech patterns I used when channeling. I examined the channeled ideas that had come through me, to see if they really contrasted with my own. I listened to several tapes in succession and noticed how each session built on the one before. I discovered a body of teachings that had been systematically presented to me. Having something (an external tape) that the rational mind could comprehend helped me gain confidence in my channeling efforts.

2. Keep a journal or record of your channeling.

Even if you channel consciously, you may find it difficult to remember much of what your guide has said during a channeling session—particularly a few days later. If you take notes immediately after channeling, you will produce an external record that can help you gain confidence in the quality and integrity of the teachings you have received. If you are able to write down your conversations with guides as you have them, you will have a complete record available to study later. This process of directly transcribing channeled conversations is called automatic writing.

3. Practice with people who know you well.

If you have friends or family who are open to channeling, try to channel for them sometimes. Channeling for other people requires you to act as an intermediary while your friends interact with your guides. They can ask questions of a personal or more universal nature, and hear your guide's perspective. Receiving other people's honest feedback on what they have seen happening can help build your confidence in the integrity of channeling. Also, as you discover yourself channeling information that you had no previous knowledge of, you will lend new credence to the quality of the information you are receiving. A word of advice:

don't perform your initial channelings for people who
are extremely skeptical. The negative biases of others
can only reinforce your own doubts.

A Special Note to Nonverbal Channels

I have written about the problems of addressing
one's doubts primarily from the point of view of a
verbal channel. Nonverbal channels, however, share
many of the same basic issues. Like verbal channels,
you may doubt the whole channeling process and fear
that it is "merely imagination." Depending on the type
of channeling you do, you may feel more or less
uncertainty.

If, as a nonverbal channel, you channel music or
artistic images when tuning in to guidance, you will
find the task of addressing your doubts much easier
than some others do. Once you have drawn or painted
the images you've seen, once you have played or
scored the music you've heard, the art and the music
will stand on their own merits. The issue of whether
you are making it up becomes moot in the process of
artistic creation. If your nonverbal channeling takes this
form, the intrinsic beauty of the imagery and the process of translating it into artistic forms takes prece-
dence over questions of their ultimate origin. The primary concern in this kind of channeling is to keep
allowing the images to come through and to keep
expressing them by putting them into form.

Other kinds of nonverbal channeling, as described
in Chapter Seven, may raise more serious doubts.
These channels may receive visual images that have
healing properties or that contain lessons hidden within them. The fact that these experiences do not always
convey a clear meaning can increase the channel's
doubts. For instance, the student whose guide kept
changing costumes often wondered about the meaning
of these transformations. I interpreted it as a lesson
that taught the channel to avoid becoming attached to
any particular form of teaching and to remain open and
receptive to whatever comes. My student eventually

adopted this interpretation as his own, and he started to recognize the value of this lesson. However, before he could reach this point, he had to watch these channeled images patiently over a long period of time. Generally speaking, a nonverbal channel always needs to ask, "Why am I receiving this imagery? What does it have to teach me?"

The same fundamental guidelines apply in assessing the relevance of nonverbal channeled material. Does the act of channeling this material feel healing and nourishing to you? Do these channelings teach you something that you need to know? If you answer these questions positively, then continue with your channeling. If you find no value in these teachings, however, then it is foolish for you to continue.

Committing Time to Channel

Channeled relationships resemble all others. If you lavish attention on them, they thrive; if you ignore them, they wither. Many of the people I have taught to channel have had profound first encounters with their guides. Some people, after experiencing deep emotions they associated with "coming home," have even wept with joy. Nevertheless, when I meet these same people six months later, they have often had no further contact with their guides. Even though they usually claim they want to "get back" to it, they haven't set aside the time to develop this aspect of their lives.

Your guides will continue to love and direct you regardless of whether you channel or not. However, if you want to make this interaction a more conscious part of your life, you must commit yourself to channeling regularly. How much time is the right amount? Only you can know that, but I would suggest that you contact your guide at least once a week—just as often as you might try to keep in touch with any good friend. This doesn't mean you have to restrict yourself to any set time. Just select a time when you feel relaxed and undistracted. The concept of spending quality time applies to guides as well as human beings.

My own experience with channeling demonstrates that you don't need to make a regular appointment to contact your guide. When I first began, I channeled every day for months, partially to convince myself that this strange phenomenon was really happening. After this initial immersion in the experience, I went through a phase where I wanted to pay more attention to my outer world, and therefore channeled infrequently—once every two or three weeks. Now I channel for ten to forty-five minutes every two or three days. I channel when I'm going through a crisis and need guidance, or when I just want contact. I love my spirit friends and begin to miss them, just as I miss my human friends when we are out of touch for too long. Sometimes I just tune in to feel their presence.

One of my best friends has formed an extremely deep relationship with his guide. His guide communicates simple directives which tell him what he needs to learn next to further his spiritual development. When he has completed that teaching, his guide reappears with another simple directive. Although they have very little actual contact, this relationship has transformed my friends's life.

Follow your own inclination about how much you want to channel. Confer with your guide about the amount of time that he or she feels is appropriate. Just make sure to put in enough time to build this unique and highly rewarding relationship.

Building a Support System

For most channels, finding a support system that will encourage them in their channeling efforts is crucial. I know channeling teachers in many parts of the country who run support groups for their students. People whom I have taught to channel have spontaneously formed their own support groups. These groups provide many important benefits. On the most basic level, they offer people the opportunity to practice channeling and to strengthen their skill. They also reinforce the importance of intuitive consciousness—

which our society, by and large, discourages. Finally, these groups provide a network of friends who can share this new interest with you.

You may also build this support system on a more intimate level by inviting your partner or a close friend to channel with you. I know many couples who share channeling experiences. They may channel once a week or once a month for each other. Or they may never channel for each other, but instead share their individual channeling experiences. Incorporating channeling as part of your relationship will weave it into the fabric of your life, making it an integral part of your daily experience.

When I first channeled Diya, he spoke to me about my concept of family. He showed me that I had limited myself and that I needed to welcome plants, animals, and discarnate beings as well as humans into my family. He instructed me, "Make your family a vertical family extending into other dimensions, as well as a horizontal family including other earth beings." Like so much of the information I have channeled, this notion was initially alien to me. However, over time my partner and I have accepted our spirit friends as part of our family. We try to channel at least once a week together. These channelings focus on getting our guides' perspectives on different life situations, on how we can use them to grow and prosper. For instance, we recently thought about moving to Boulder, Colorado. Our guides helped us make a decision by sharing their perspectives of the pros and cons of this move—the aspects of ourselves that this move would help develop and the experience we hoped to gain in making it. They also gave us practical suggestions about completing our lives in Los Angeles.

When we want to address important topics, we each channel our own guides. We will also channel each other's guides. I might channel Walter, my partner's guide, for a few minutes; my partner will then complete the channeling. By changing the channel in mid-channeling, we can then compare notes, giving us a chance to see if we both receive similar information.

I also call on my guides for help when I experience

stress in my relationship with my partner. They offer me their perspectives on the difficulty and suggestions on how best to deal with it. They tend to zero in on ways I can change my responses and reactions to make the relationship work better. They often advise me to refocus away from troubled areas and to concentrate instead on areas that work well in order to give the relationship a chance to grow in an unpressured way. Both my partner and I love our guides and feel that they provide important support to us as individuals and as a couple. Sharing the channeling experience with a partner has enriched the meaning of family for me and has given me the support I needed to develop more rapport with my guides.

Even if you are unable to interest your partner in channeling, you will find other friends willing to share this experience with you. If you can find a friend interested in channeling and who wants to learn with you, it will make the process more real and satisfying. If they express an interest, fine; but don't try to convert them if they don't. This can only create distance between you and them. If your current friends show no interest in channeling, but you remain focused yourself on this new interest, you will unquestionably attract new friends who can share this phenomenon with you. This is the law of sympathetic attraction.

As you considered the three factors that can help build a good relationship with your guide—addressing your doubts, committing time, and building a support system—you may have noticed how interrelated they are. You will find it easier to work through doubts when you have committed time to channeling and you have friends who support you and share their similar doubts. You will make time for channeling more readily when you refuse to allow hidden doubts to drive you away from the experience, and when you have friends with whom you can share the experience, since most people avoid pursuing socially isolating experiences. Finally, you will find the support you need more quickly when you have firmly decided that you want to commit time to channeling.

Channeling is a simple skill to learn, but it challenges many of our notions of the world. It takes courage to challenge our old ideas of the universe and our limited assessments of our own capabilities. It takes persistence to redirect our focus from externally rewarded outer experiences to more subtle inner experiences. But if you follow the guidelines in this chapter, you will ease this transition and allow your relationship with your guide to flourish.

Increasing Your Clarity as a Channel

As you have just seen, you can take several steps that will help build a relationship with your guide. As you develop this relationship over time, an important facet of the relationship will involve increasing your clarity and receptivity as a channel.

Earlier in this chapter I described the way we translate the energetic resonance of our guides into our own words and concepts; we filtered the guides' perspectives through our own vocabulary and constructs. In this sense, channeled information always springs from a unique marriage between our being and that of our spirit friends. Channeled information is therefore never pure or "uncontaminated." However, although we always translate channeled information, our translations admit varying degrees of purity and clarity. Just as human translators vary in their ability to transmit meaning and essence accurately, channels vary in their ability to relay their guides' teachings accurately.

In determining the purity or the clarity of the channeling, perhaps the most important quality is the channel's detachment from the material. When you ask a question, if you already know what answer you want to hear, you may unwittingly distort the information by allowing your own conscious or unconscious material to color your channeling. On the other hand, when you channel information that you have no strong investment in, you will most likely channel with less distortion.

Does this mean that you should never channel information that has any sort of personal meaning to you? Of course not. You can channel material that addresses any issue. However, if you have a personal stake in the material you are channeling, exercise caution if the channeled material begins to sound like a record of your deepest desires.

Highly evolved guides generally avoid giving you material that will placate you by predicting that your every dream will come true. Generally they transmit material that will dislodge you from your own limitations and difficulties. A good channeling usually includes an element of surprise and offers you new ways of looking at your situation. As you attempt to assess the clarity of your own channeling, ask yourself whether you are receiving new ideas that challenge and expand you. If you feel that you might be distorting the material, stop the channeling, center yourself in your vase, and begin the channeling again. If you receive the same information, this may indicate that you are bringing the information through clearly. However, if you still sense that you may be distorting, put aside channeling on this issue until you have become more detached from the possible results.

Of course, the ultimate way of assessing the clarity of your own channeling is to put this material into practice in your life and observe its effects. If, like Thom Elkjer and Darryl Anka, you learn specific principles that transform the quality of your life in a positive way, you will learn to trust the clarity of your channeling. If you receive predictive information from your guides that proves to be accurate, your trust in your own clarity will increase. The manner in which your channeled information affects your life offers you the best feedback on the quality and clarity of your channeling. As you clearly observe the positive results of channeled wisdom, feelings of trust in your guides and in yourself as a channel will increase.

Chapter Nine

Learning Special Channeling Techniques

Channeling spirit guides, as I wrote in Chapter One, is just one specialized application of channeling. The more general process of resonance, however, can be directed anywhere. By focusing resonance in other directions, you can practice a variety of specialized channeling techniques. Some of these techniques involve specialized usages of verbally channeling guides, while others require you to concentrate the channeling ability elsewhere.

Don't feel obligated to try any of these techniques. I offer them only as options which you may choose to explore or not, depending on your own interests and curiosity. If you do decide to practice these techniques, however, you may derive several benefits. On the most fundamental level, you will experience the sheer joy of expanding your own awareness and sensitivity. The very human delight in self-mastery and exploration—most evident in small children—remains forever alive in us to some degree. As you learn to use your channeling abilities in new ways, you will feel an increase in your own sense of personal power and in your own abilities to respond sensitively to the world. As you learn to channel different types of energy and intelligence, you will also find your sense of alienation and isolation decreasing. For ultimately, channeling is merely a process of resonance and expression. As you resonate to more and more aspects of life, you will feel more and more connected to those aspects in particular and to life in general.

Experimenting with specialized techniques will also allow you to explore your own natural gifts and tendencies. Each individual develops his or her own unique way of becoming a channel or conduit for other levels of awareness. If you practice channeling your spirit guides verbally and find that you meet with limited success, you may possess a sensitivity that can best utilize another approach. An axiom which applies to psychic work of any kind states that it is best to travel along the path of least resistance, to find the natural style and focus of your psychic awareness and work on developing it. Experimenting with different techniques will help you investigate your own natural abilities.

Channeling Your Guides for Other People

As you strengthen your relationship with your guides, you may find other people attracted to that aspect of your life. They may express their interest by asking you questions about your experience or by requesting that you teach them how to channel. But they may also reveal their curiosity by asking you to channel your guides for them.

Many people would like to make contact with the spirit world and obtain a fresh perspective on their lives, but they don't want to take the time to develop this skill themselves. Or perhaps they feel that they lack the ability to develop this skill. Many professional channels provide services to people who fit into this category. Some of your friends might fit this description too, and they may approach you to do a channeling for them.

When you channel your guides for other people, although you employ the same process, you do so with the intention of acting as an intermediary between your friends and your guides. Your guides will speak to your friends through you, addressing any personal ques-

ons or any cosmological questions they might pose.
eople generally ask guides questions that revolve around
heir relationships with others or around work—the
wo primary arenas of human experience and learning.

When you channel for others, follow all the initial
teps in the same manner—relaxing, invoking your
uide, grounding and merging with your vase. Once
ou have entered your trance state, however, instead of
nitiating a direct dialogue with your guide and asking
our own questions, let the people you are channeling
or ask their questions. As the channel, you will speak
our guide's response aloud, so that a conversation can
evelop between your guide and your friends.

Doing a channeling for others can produce many
enefits for both you and your friends. Your friends can
tilize the perspectives of your guides in the same way
ou do: they will learn new ways of looking at things and
ew ways of dealing with life more effectively. Just the
xperience of receiving information in this unique way
vill probably expand your friends' ideas about the es-
ence of life and the guidance available to them.

You as the channel can benefit also. Channeling
our guides for others may permit you to see your
riends in a new way. As we get to know people, we
ften develop rigid ideas of who they are and who they
ren't. Of course, they contribute to these limited per-
eptions by revealing themselves selectively. But the
hanneling situation may offer your friends the oppor-
unity to reveal themselves more honestly and openly
s they ask for guidance. In addition, your guide's
nsights may provide you and your friends with a new
nderstanding of one another. Sanaya Roman, for ex-
mple, told me that channeling Orin has taught her to
ee the beauty of the soul beneath the personality.
Although you might not have such a transformational
xperience, you will certainly gain new perspectives
nd deeper understanding of people.

Channeling for others may also increase your own
earning by allowing you to listen to guidance presented
o others. Despite our obvious differences, we human
eings are alike in many fundamental ways. We share

the same joys and the same suffering. When guides offer help to a specific person in a particular situation their advice almost always applies to the human condition in general. In hearing perceptive viewpoints which concern another person's life, our own wisdom thus increases. I have picked up many valuable perspectives in listening to my guides' words to others. For instance, someone once came to ask my guides when she would meet her soul mate. She defined her soul mate as the *one* special being to whom she was bound by many incarnations and by a deep soul bond. My guides began to talk to her about the soul-mate concept as it is commonly used now. They informed her that we in fact have many soul mates, many old friends whom we are bound to by past life experiences and deep love. They told her that anytime we share deep love or resonance with another—whether that other is a lover, friend, parent child, or colleague—we become mated with that person in a moment of deep communion or sharing. They encouraged her not to think so exclusively about finding the one soul mate, but rather to make herself more receptive to the many wonderful connections of love, the many soul mates around her. Listening to this advice fascinated me, transforming my whole concept of soul mates.

Whenever you channel for friends, you might want to tape the session. This will give your friends a record of the dialogue; they may want to refer back to it at some later date. As a final aside, I would suggest that you not channel for someone else until you have built up the ability to channel for at least twenty minutes for yourself. Until you have increased your stamina—the psychic endurance that builds as you practice channeling—it is best to avoid pushing yourself by channeling too long for someone else. Just pay attention to your own limits, and you will know if and when the time is right to experiment with this technique.

Channeling Other People's Guides for Them

Once you have learned to channel one guide, you have the capability of channeling many guides. You only need to resonate to different guides and let that resonance express itself through you. You may, however, encounter certain natural obstacles that limit the guides you can channel. Some guides exist in worlds that vibrate at such a high frequency that humans find it difficult to channel them. Whenever I experimented with channeling these high-frequency guides, my body felt electrified or I began to shake. After the channeling concluded, I felt as if I had drunk ten cups of coffee. Although I am glad I discovered the existence of such beings, I don't try to channel them anymore, because the experience put such a strain on my body. Similarly, you might meet a guide whose "feel" or viewpoint you don't like. Although I have never experienced these negative sensations in relating to a guide, the possibility certainly exists. By your own choice or limitation, you might not want to channel these guides. However, even after excluding them, you still have a wide range of guides and energies available for your channeling.

Some people may ask you to channel their guides for the same reasons that they ask you to channel your guides for them. They may desire additional perspectives on their lives. However, they may feel that the guidance will be more attuned to their situation or more accurate if it comes from their own guides rather than yours. In addition, they might want to make a conscious connection with their guides without learning to channel themselves.

The channel can derive many benefits from channeling another's guides. Perhaps most importantly, the experience validates the existence of spirit guides. If I had only channeled one guide, I quite honestly would have had serious doubts about the nature of channeling. But channeling other people's guides has given me first-hand experience of many different energies, personalities, and viewpoints. This exposure has strengthened my belief that guides exist as independent entities rather than as aspects of our own individual consciousness.

Channeling other people's guides can also create a greater sense of connectedness with other dimensions of experience. Just as knowing people in different countries makes us feel connected with other parts of the world, meeting guides from different realms can create a sense of participating in a vast network of experience.

A final and very simple benefit of channeling other people's guides is that the experience can be fascinating. If you like meeting and interacting with different kinds of human beings, you will probably enjoy interacting with diverse guides.

The process involved in channeling other people's guides is almost identical to that of channeling your own guides. Begin with the usual relaxation exercises and grounding, then merge with your vase. However, instead of invoking your own guide, invoke the highest and most beneficial guides of your friend to speak through you. You might do this by repeating a prayer like, "I ask for the information that will serve the highest good of all to come through me, and for the most appropriate and loving guide of this person to be with me now."

When you feel ready to channel, use the technique outlined in Chapter Six of speaking aloud *as if* you were the guide—except in this case speak as if you were your friend's guide. This "as if" technique creates an identification between you and your friend's guide that will facilitate the channeling.

Again, as with all these techniques, experiment with this process of channeling other guides only if it matches the direction of your curiosity and interest. Three of the four channels I interviewed for this book enjoy intensely personal relationships with one guide. If you share their approach to channeling, which values relationships and constancy more than diversity, you may not want to develop the radio-receiver approach, which tunes in to different beings by changing channels.

Photo-Reading

Photo-reading, another specialized form of channeling, differs in significant ways from channeling guides. To begin with, photo-reading utilizes a symbol or representation of the entity you want to channel in order to access the perspectives of that being. When we channel a spirit guide, we resonate directly with that entity without using an intermediary. When we photo-read, we tune in to the larger energy pattern of a being by resonating with the photograph, which represents a smaller image of that larger energy pattern.

The other obvious distinction is that in photo-reading you can only channel beings who were—or are—capable of being photographed, beings who currently live on this planet or have lived here before. Thus in turning to photo-reading, we have moved into the realm of channeling other human beings.

I began to photo-read somewhat indirectly. Clients started to ask me if I wanted them to bring photographs to their psychic readings. After hearing this question a number of times, I decided that photo-reading was something I wanted to explore. I found the idea of using photographs quite pleasing since I love to study the way people look and the way they express themselves visually. When I first experimented with photo-reading, I also discovered that the photographs cued me into their beings in a very distinct way and that I could channel them quite clearly.

The procedure used to photo-read follows the same pattern as other channeling techniques. Perform your relaxation exercises, and ground and merge with your vase. Then focus your attention on the photograph you should be holding in your hand. Again using the first person identification technique, begin to speak as if you were the person in the photograph. For instance, you might say, "I am Jane. I have a pain in my chest. It seems to be connected with the loss of a child."

As with all channeling, you will experience a moment when you simply open up and begin to say the words that come to you whether you understand them rationally or not. The channeling process involves trust in your own ability to tune in and bring forth the perspective of the being you're channeling. Every psychic and every conscious channel I know has experienced this moment of the intuitive leap—the moment that you jump from your rational thinking to intuitive perception. The trust that you can make that leap grows with time and practice, but the leap itself never disappears. If you plan to do any intuitive work, you will have to trust your own abilities and begin to speak or channel from the nonrational part of yourself.

In recent years neurologists have conducted a good deal of research on brain lateralization. The left hemisphere is apparently connected with logic, linear thinking, and analysis, while the right side of the brain is the center for intuitive, holistic thought. I believe that the intuitive leap every channel or psychic experiences in fact represents the movement of consciousness from the left side of the brain to the right side of the brain. A neurological leap accompanies the experiential leap.

Photo-reading can increase your understanding of others and extend your resonating abilities to other human beings. In addition, channeling other human beings offers you a unique opportunity to assess the accuracy of your channeling. Since no one really knows spirit guides, we have no way of evaluating the accuracy of our translation of their messages. But by photo-reading a friend's sister or husband, you can often receive some feedback about the precision of your channeling. If you make a tape of the session and allow your friend to play it for the person you channeled, you can receive even more precise feedback—from the subject of your photo-reading.

The person who asks you to do a photo-reading will gain the opportunity to increase his or her understanding, and perhaps to heal a damaged relationship through this kind of channeling. Maybe your friend directs a great deal of blame toward an abusive father. If you channel this father, your friend may develop a new understanding of the motivations underlying the father's behavior, and this new understanding may free him or her from a repetitive and useless blaming of the father.

Although I have enjoyed photo-reading and demonstrating this ability to myself, I do not intend to pursue it. When a psychic "reads" or does a psychic reading of another, he or she scans that person with the inner senses. The psychic feels the personality and the larger being of an individual and translates this information through imagery and physical sensation, inner sounds and smells. However, in order to channel another human being, you have to merge your own energy system more completely with that of the person being channeled and allow that resonance to be expressed through your own body. You may talk in the first person, using the mannerisms of the person being channeled.

This kind of resonating can prove tiresome and even unpleasant when the person you channel is not particularly loving or self-aware. When I channel guides, I only work with beings who express a very light, loving energy. When you channel human beings who identify themselves by their own suffering, your body feels their suffering too. And if they have a limited understanding of their lives, you temporarily experience that limited understanding . To avoid these problems, try to establish a link with the higher self of an individual whenever you channel a human being. You can accomplish this by saying a prayer—that you want to channel the highest aspect of this being that you are capable of channeling, in order to gain the greatest illumination in the situation.

About a year ago, I experienced a relatively unpleasant instance of photo-channeling. A woman came to me and asked me to channel her lover, who had died in her bed of a heart attack while she was away. As I tuned in to him through a photograph, I found myself talking almost obsessively about karma and paying back mistakes in one life through learning situations in a subsequent life. Since I do not subscribe to this belief and view it as restrictive, I found the experience of being inside that kind of thinking somewhat unpleasant. When I had completed the channeling, I apologized to my client for framing her reading in these concepts, assuring her that I didn't really subscribe to that viewpoint. "But my lover did," she said, "and he spoke of it in almost identical terms." Although I felt gratified at being able to accurately channel someone who had recently died, the experience itself wasn't particularly pleasant.

If you would like to do photo-readings, I would advise you to experiment with it in a limited fashion. Perhaps you have a talent for it and can help yourself and other people to understand their significant others through this technique. Perhaps your body will not react as sensitively to the experience as mine did. I know many fine channels who have a stronger physical constitution than I do, who can channel for longer periods of time and channel some energies more easily than I can. However, I would still advise you to be aware of your own sensitivities and talents when experimenting with this technique.

Psychometry

Psychometry is the channeling of information or subtle energies through attunement to objects. Every object carries its own electromagnetic vibrations. By resonating to these vibrations, we can tune in to various levels of information or energy.

Several times in this book, I have pointed to our ability to resonate to anything. One application of psychometry entails tuning in to an object to understand experientially the beingness of that object. Another approach involves resonating with an object in order to channel information about someone connected with that object.

Let's look first at the idea of resonating to the properties of an object simply to understand the beingness of that object. At first you might wonder why anyone would want to tune in to an inanimate object such as a rock. One reason you might try it is to connect yourself more fully with the world around you. We are surrounded by things we consider dead or unalive. And once we relegate something to the unalive or dead category, we often ignore it. We remove our conscious awareness from it. As a result, we are insensitive to many of the things that surround us. We regard large portions of our world as dead, not so much because they are dead, but because we do not attend to them. Resonating to a rock or a body of water, feeling its qualities, can wake us up to the world around us and bring it to life. Heightening our sensitivity in this way enriches our world.

To channel an object such as a rock, prepare yourself for channeling by relaxing, and grounding, and merging with your vase. Then, instead of attuning to your guides, focus on the rock you hold in your hand or, if it is too large to hold, just touch it. Allow yourself to receive the impressions of your inner senses as you resonate to the rock. You may feel very old, or feel your body slowing down and becoming more dense. Don't anticipate any particular experience as you try to feel what "rockness" is like. Just observe your own experience. If you want to express this experience verbally, you can externalize it using the "I" technique.

Obviously rocks cannot deliver eloquent, elaborate messages in the same way spirit guides do, but they can teach us certain qualities of being by simply exhibiting their essential nature. When you hold a rock in your hand, you might be able to feel its slower vibratory pattern. To many people who love rocks, this slowness and density offers a relief from the faster movement of our own metabolic process. When I hold a rock in my hand, I learn something about slowing down and being more patient. Sometimes I will hold a rock when I need to slow myself down and become more stable and less impatient. I know other people who hold rocks to remind themselves of the importance of emotional solidity and stability.

Psychometry can also be used like photo-reading, to attune to the owner of an object. Just as the scent of people lingers in their clothing, their subtle energies become infused into the objects they keep close to them. Objects that have a lot of contact with the person being read—a wedding ring or a favorite necklace—are commonly used for channeling.

Again as with photo-reading, follow the usual procedures that prepare you for channeling. However, instead of resonating to your guide, resonate to the person who is connected with the object. Again, by using the first person and speaking as if you were the owner of the object, you will establish an identification that will allow you to express that person's viewpoints and experience.

Psychometry, like photo-reading, is a technique used by many kinds of psychics. For instance, some police forces use psychics to locate missing persons. And these psychics sometimes employ psychometric techniques to help them tune in to the whereabouts of the missing person. However, although both psychics and channels use psychometry to stimulate paranormal awareness, the psychic uses the inner senses to gather information about the person being read and then integrates this information into descriptions. The channel uses his or her own body to express the experience of the person being channeled.

In its broadest sense, you could say that channeling is a psychic or intuitive ability. And in its broadest sense, you could say that psychic work is channeling in that it acts as a mediary between subtle levels of perception and the external world. However, differences in approach and technique distinguish these styles of intuitive work from one another.

Channeling and Art

A very special form of channeling is the channeling of art, either visual imagery or music or dance. Many artists have discussed the way their dance dances them or their music writes itself. In the introduction, I referred to the movie *Amadeus*, comparing the experience of channeling to the way Mozart's music poured through him and distinguished itself from his coarse personality.

Creative people in all fields of endeavor have described how the solution to an artistic or scientific problem that stymied all of their rational powers came in a flash of insight or in a dream; in decidedly nonrational ways. In these kinds of situations, people almost feel as if they had been overtaken by a creative solution, as if their conscious ego was no longer in control. In many ways this sounds like channeling, and it *is* channeling in its broadest sense of bringing information and energy from more expanded states of awareness into the material plane.

Although creative people may have always used channeling to some degree in their work, individuals are now beginning to create the channeling state *consciously* in order to bring through creative imagery and inspiration. Just as people learn to channel in order to bring forth information and energy from more expanded states of consciousness, visionary artists are now utilizing meditative states to open themselves to imagery that evokes a high level of wisdom. They then translate those images into concrete visual form through painting or drawing. Since I have never channeled images, I interviewed two channeling artists to hear what they had to say about channeling visual images.

Carole Hoss, a visionary artist who lives in Los Angeles, has painted a series of animals which have been made into greeting cards and posters. More recently she has painted pictures of beings from other dimensions, and of light and energies from other dimensions as they interact with the physical world.

Carole told me that when she paints her realistic art, she studies the object at great length until she understands the feeling or the spiritual nature of it. She then proceeds to paint the picture in great detail. However, when she paints her visionary art, she uses a meditative or dream state as the starting point. The image that she receives, only partially visual, has more of a feeling structure than a visual one. When she paints this kind of picture, she feels energy pouring down through a long tunnel of energy into the right hemisphere of her brain. When she begins to translate this feeling image to the canvas, she follows intuitive instructions like, "Move your brush to the right," rather than trying to re-create an external image.

> When I get into my visionary work, it's like
> I'll all of a sudden move in a certain way, and my
> mind will say, "Oh, there it is." My mind is

following, not leading. That's why I feel they paint themselves. At a certain point they just take off. When they're done, I look at them and think, "Gee that's really good. I really like that one." Some of them are like that. They aren't even mine in a sense, and yet they are mine, from another level of myself. In that sense you can call them channeled.

Judith Cornell, a Marin County artist, also considers her art to be channeled. She goes into a deep meditative state with the intention of accessing imagery that will bring beauty and peace to the earth. This method can be understood as an analogous process to the vase technique, which you have learned to use to access information and energies from expanded states of awareness—your own or your guide's.

> *For me it involves getting into a deep meditative state of unconditional love and thinking about images that will inspire and bring about beauty, peace, and healing to the planet. My intention is to bring in higher inspiration, and my experience of it is very profound. It is very different from the work I did years ago, which was based on the lower levels of imagination and outward observation.*

In teaching people to channel art, Judith first guides her students into a relaxed state. Then she asks them to visualize a rainbow spectrum of light streaming through their bodies. While they are still in a relaxed, meditative state, she tells them to imagine themselves in a Hall of Wisdom where they can speak to their higher self or their guides. She instructs them to bring back inspirational images from their encounters with guides or expanded parts of themselves. Judith reported that her students bring back beautiful visions from this experience. Finally, she teaches them standard academic design and color techniques so they can draw and paint their visions.

In her forthcoming book, *The Creative Powers within You: Keys to Awakening the Artist in Everyone,* Judith displays beautifully crafted, inspirational art done by students with little previous knowledge of art or of meditation. Judith perceives channeled art as closely related to the evolution of consciousness:

> *I feel that the new vision is the power that lies within each of us. To go to that higher level of visualization is to bring peace and beauty, not only to art, but to the scientific community. We are on the verge of a new age, if people could just bring their imaginations and vibratory levels to that higher frequency. This is where our salvation comes from, not from external, but from internal vision.*

A Final Word on Special Channeling Techniques

The world of channeling is an extremely rich and varied one. Once you have learned to ground yourself and temporarily suspend the rule of your personality, you can send your consciousness in many different directions and bring back new information, energies, and perceptions from the subtle dimensions of the universe. I believe that in the not-too-distant future the word channeling will be obsolete: movement between different states of awareness will be fluid and easily navigated. As all of us—as individuals and as a culture—become more aware and more accustomed to these abilities, they will become an integral part of our perception.

Just as children know and value these abilities in themselves, we as individuals will learn to tune in to the nonphysical sources of creativity most appropriate to our own unique creativity. We will learn to express our unique linkage to expanded awareness in our own individual ways. I believe that we are moving into a time when these specialized channeling techniques will be acknowledged as the birthright of all people.

Chapter Ten

Channeling and the Evolution of Consciousness

I would like to close this book by looking at the potential effects of channeling on our individual and collective consciousness. In particular, I would like to look at the impact channeling may have on our religious, scientific, and psychological views of ourselves. If we as individuals and as a race are in the process of evolving toward more expanded, more refined levels of awareness—and I believe we are—then what role does channeling play in this evolution?

Channeling and Spirituality

During one of my recent lectures on channeling, a very intelligent Israeli woman asked me how I thought channeling and traditional religions fit together. She especially wanted to know why so many people today seem to be turning away from traditional religions and seeking alternative forms of spiritual exploration such as channeling. I think this woman's question echoes the thoughts of millions of people throughout the world.

We live in a historical period and a part of the world where people have the freedom to question the meaning of their lives. We have the political right to do so, and as a society, we have a large enough food supply to ensure that our thoughts are not constantly on survival.

During the sixties a relatively affluent American generation turned its attention to questions of meaning. Certainly every generation has produced its political dissidents, its spiritual seekers, and its social avant-garde, but the sixties gave birth to a mass movement of young people who challenged the political, social, and spiritual status quo.

When young people turned their attention to spiritual matters, they found answers that didn't have much relevance to them. Judaism and Christianity told stories about people in archaic cultures who seemed to have achieved direct communication with God. These religions offered moral prescriptions on how to lead a good life, but did not provide the means of duplicating the communion with God that these past prophets and masters experienced. Ritual and moral prescription without any inner corroborative experience of spiritual truth seemed empty and meaningless to a generation hungry for truth and impatient with platitudes. In addition to disillusionment with the spiritual content religion offered, many of the more politically minded pointed out the coercive role of religions in helping oppressed peoples to accept unacceptable political and social situations.

Since traditional religions were failing to meet their needs, many people turned toward alternatives that would allow them to experience spiritual realities more directly. LSD and other consciousness-expanding drugs were one of the first methods used to explore expanded states of consciousness. But when the physical and emotional hazards of these drugs became apparent, and when people started to realize that you always come down from a drug-induced high, this generation of spiritual seekers began to turn to other technologies that would encourage their exploration of consciousness.

The first wave of spiritual technologies used in the United States were imported. The influx of great spiritual masters from the East began at the turn of the twentieth century. However, as the hunger for these teachings increased during the sixties and seventies, many sects based on ancient yogic and Buddhist teachings found their way to the West. Meditation and Hatha Yoga offered specific methodologies for achieving inner states of serenity, balance, and for opening more subtle dimensions of experience. These teachings implicitly presented a picture of the human being as an entity capable of achieving states of unconditional love and awareness of our multidimensional selves.

Channeling is another methodology that allows us to tap more directly into other dimensions of experience and become more aware of our multidimensional beings. Channeling also gives us access to teachers who can monitor our spiritual development and help us move into greater states of awareness. Channeling is very much part of the trend toward increasing personal visionary experience and the acceptance of personal intuitive experience evident in this country since the sixties.

Let's return now to that woman's question about how traditional religions and channeling fit together. It is important to note that while channeling in one sense developed in response to the general disillusionment with traditional religions in the West, it does not preclude traditional religions. In fact, the two potentially have much to offer each other.

Traditional religions provide a structure for likeminded people to come together and place their lives in a spiritual context. Traditional religions provide rituals that make sacred major life transitions—birth, puberty, marriage, and death. Traditional role models provide us with images of individuals who have benefited from divine guidance and achieved states of unconditional love through their own spiritual struggles. These intrinsically human needs for community and example cannot be satisfied through channeling or meditation or any technology that opens us to inner experience.

On the other hand, traditional Western religions do not offer us the means to develop our own mystical, visionary capacity. Judaism and Christianity provide moral precepts and religious ritual, but these prescrip-

ions for good works rarely produce individual visionary experience. In fact, traditional religions often suggest that these inner mystical experiences belong
exclusively to the original teachers and leaders of the
sect or to rare saints and sages. Traditional religions
often maintain their own power by suggesting that
their particular masters had the one direct line to God
and that those leaders have acted as unique channels
for the wisdom and teaching of God.

The phenomenon of channeling does not downplay
the spiritual achievements of the masters who have
gone before. Channeling implicitly says, "Do not merely imitate the actions of the great masters. Love them,
honor them, and achieve the same inner realities that
produced those actions." Channeling tells us, "There is
much more to our selves than our personalities. We can
contact many dimensions of experience. We ourselves
have many dimensions of being. Jesus was not the only
son of God. The prophets were not the only chosen
ones. We are all chosen ones, and we are all sons and
daughters of God."

There can be no doubt that channeling does have
radical implications, for it democratizes spirituality. It
offers every person access to spiritual guidance and
revelation. To the degree traditional religions can em-
brace that democracy and encourage the individual
intuitive process, it is possible for a new, revitalized
spirituality to emerge within traditional religious forms.
If traditional religions can integrate new technologies
into their community structures, they can offer a great
support for spiritual seekers, and become enlivened
and updated themselves.

Channeling and the Scientific Paradigm

Throughout this book I have explored the ways in
which growing up in a scientifically based culture limits our ideas of what is real. As more and more people
gain first-hand experience of subtle realities and other
dimensions of experience, we must confront a potential
erosion or shift in our prevailing cultural model. Our

increased sensitivity to the worlds of the inner sense
and trust in intuition have accelerated our growing
understanding that the outer senses comprise only one
of our available systems for experiencing and knowing.

You may have noticed a parallel here between the
scientific paradigm and traditional religions. The phenomenon of channeling does not negate or preclude
traditional religious structures. But it does imply that
there is much more to the average human being than
traditional religions have recognized. Similarly, the phenomenon of channeling does not preclude the truths of
the outer senses or of scientific realities. But channeling does imply that the scientific model fails to account
for every dimension of truth. Just as the electron micro-
scope has challenged our scientific understanding by
proving that our apparently solid world is in fact a
dance of subatomic particles, channeling as another
kind of tool also defies a strictly materialist view of the
universe. Channeling teaches us that the nature of
reality shifts depending on the perceptual tool used to
perceive it, and that many bands of reality are accessible to different instruments and modes of human
perception.

Jonathan Klimo, a former Rutgers University professor, is an interdisciplinary researcher and writer who
recently published a book entitled *Channeling: Investigations on Receiving Information from Paranormal Sources.*
Klimo holds that at any given time in any culture, a
shared or consensual reality defines the worldview of
that culture. In a recent personal interview, he told me

> *Always one is dealing with consensual reality.*
> *That is what is agreed to by the majority of people*
> *in a community or culture as the shared experience*
> *of and belief in what is objectively or primarily real.*
> *Yet the nature of a given consensual reality is*
> *subject to change. Just look at the history of this*
> *planet, its history of ideas, the development of its*
> *science, the evolutionary shifts, and the cycles of con-*

*sensus regarding which mythic belief system is held
dominant by the people.*

Professor Klimo delineates several of these consensual realities that have held sway over human history. He talks of the materialist view that sees mind as a secondary phenomenon, a lesser reality, coming out of the bioelectrical activity of a physical brain. This viewpoint has been predominant in the Western world since the Enlightenment. According to this belief, consciousness is a product of the physical brain, and if the brain ceases to exist, so does our consciousness.

In recent years Klimo has noted an acceleration of "bleed throughs" from, or crosstalk with, other realities. For example, many people have begun to report out-of-body experiences and near-death experiences in which they have been aware of their immediate environments although they were clinically dead. Like channeling, the proliferation of these experiences challenges the materialist worldview and raises two possibilities for understanding: a dualistic position that maintains mind and matter are distinct, that matter exists independent of consciousness and consciousness independent of matter; or a mentalist position that views spirit or consciousness as the only reality and matter as merely an expression of consciousness. This echoes philosopher George Berkeley's statement that "All things are ideas in the mind of God."

Klimo believes that we are beginning to see a shift in our predominant paradigm due to the evidence offered by channeling and other experiences involving realities that cannot be called physical as currently defined.

If you define channeling as receiving information from some other level or dimension of reality, then some kind of interdimensional bleed through is taking place that doesn't involve the five senses and that transcends what we tend to think of as real. The increased incidence of channeling tells me that the paradigm is shifting and the consensus reality is in the process of modulating. What has for so long

*been taken to be the primary reality—the physical—
is going to change places with the nonphysical, the
mental and spiritual, as primary. What so much of
the channeled material has been telling us is that we
share a level of existence that is adjacent to that of
these beings [guides] who are communicating with
us, and that this takes place within a vast, multidimensional, populated cosmos which is basically one
spiritual Being. These other-dimensional neighbors,
who share our identity with this one Being, are
saying: "We are real. You are not alone. We are
coming through to show you that there is more than
physical reality and that you survive the death of
your physical body. You are an immortal spirit. You
are more than the physical." This coincides with
most prophecy as well. All of this tends to support
the contention that there will soon be a major shift
in our consensus reality, probably within our lifetimes.*

Channeling and Psychological Views of the Self

Through channeling and other intuitive experiences, our sense of who we are as beings is beginning
to shift. The first half of this century provided us with
two primary psychological models of who we are—
behaviorist and psychodynamic. Both of these models
basically see only the part of the human being conditioned by experiences in the world. Neither acknowledges the realms of intuitive experience.

The behaviorist model bypasses any kind of subjective world at all, depicting the human being as a
complex system of stimulus-response patterns. This
model claims that we have developed a complex network of programmed, automatic responses to cues. For
instance, perhaps you burnt your hand badly on a
stove as a child and now you don't like to cook. The
stimulus—in this case, burning your hand—provokes a
conditioned response—an aversion to stoves, and by
association, to cooking. This system, solely interested
in input conditioning and output behaviors, regards

any emotional reactions or intellectual interpretations that accompanied this traumatic incident as irrelevant. Anything that is neither stimulus nor response does not exist at all, according to the behaviorist model.

The psychodynamic model is perhaps the major model of human functioning today. Whereas behaviorists show no interest in subjective internal responses to external situations, psychodynamic psychologists find them fascinating. The psychodynamic model sees the human being as a battleground for conflicting aspects of the personality. This model postulates a set of primal drives—sexual and aggressive—that are partially known to us and partially cut off (unconscious) from our awareness. Opposing these primal drives are internalized social values that often run counter to our instincts. Completing this picture is the ego, which mediates between the primal drives and the social values. Integral to this system is the unconscious—the parts of our experience that our ego has cut off from conscious awareness because they conflict too much with idealized notions of ourselves and with what we can safely express in our environments.

These two systems of thought are the ones used most pervasively in mental health systems today. One system sees the human being as a mechanistic stimulus-response pattern. The other understands the human being as a dynamism of conflicting psychic components.

Channeling, clairvoyance, meditation, telepathy, precognition, and other intuitive experiences challenge the limits of these psychological models of ourselves. Although these psychological theories may brilliantly describe that aspect of our beings known as the personality, they do not begin to deal with the other levels of being, untied to physical experience.

In the past twenty-five years two new schools of psychology have begun to emerge: humanistic and transpersonal psychology. Humanistic psychology arose in the sixties as a discipline that studies human potential—creative, interpersonal, and spiritual. Humanistic psychology emphasizes understanding the human being from a nonpathological viewpoint, seeing the human being as a system continually reaching toward greater levels of creative self-expression. Transpersonal psychology, an offshoot of humanistic psychology, attempts to understand those aspects of human experience that go beyond the individual personality. Transpersonal psychology represents Western psychology's first attempt to describe and understand the multidimensional experience of the self.

However, although transpersonal psychology exists, it is by no means the most widely held viewpoint. As channeling and other intuitive experiences become more widely experienced and more widely publicized, the older psychological models will begin to expand in an attempt to incorporate this new knowledge. As intuitive experiences become more common, they will certainly add another dimension to our already excellent understanding of the personality and its functions. Just as old scientific models superbly describe one band of experience—the physical—traditional psychology brilliantly describes one aspect of consciousness—the personality. As we develop as a race, we will need a new psychological model that acknowledges the unconscious, conscious, and superconsious aspects of our selves.

A Final Note to the Reader

I hope that this excursion into channeling has broadened your sense of your own potential and of the potential of the human race in general. Whether you choose to explore channeling per se is less important than whether you gained through this book an expanded sense of who you really are. Channeling is a valuable tool in the evolution of consciousness. But it's only a tool, and as such is only appropriate to some people in some places at some times in their development. At every stage of your development you need to find the tool or method that will best open you to a greater sense of your own essential nature.

Why is this quest for your own nature so crucial? I believe that if we want our world to survive, we must make a quantum leap in consciousness. Simply changing our prevailing political or religious systems will not achieve our salvation. We have raped the earth and killed one another in the name of capitalism or communism or fascism. We have polluted our environment and maimed each other in the names of Christianity, Judaism, Hinduism, and Islam. Political structures and religions come and go, but we as a species continue to violate the earth and each other. The change must occur in us, in our essential being. Now we have upped the ante. We have created nuclear weaponry and will destroy ourselves if we do not make these fundamental changes.

In a very practical way, channeling and other intuitive arts move us a step closer to the kind of consciousness we as a race need in order to survive. As I remarked in the first pages of this book, channeling is based on extended resonance or empathy. As we develop the ability to resonate in specific channeling sessions, this sensitivity will spill into our lives in general, making us all more and more unified with and appreciative of all life. It may sound eccentric to resonate to a rock, but once you have, you will never strip mine the earth in the same unthinking way. Similar revelations arise in resonating with trees, animals, or other human beings. As our sense of unity and identification develops through different intuitive practices, it will become more difficult, if not impossible, to harm another. For we will truly know that in wounding another, we wound ourselves, and in exploiting the earth, we exploit ourselves.

I hope that this book will serve you in your individual evolution and that it will contribute to the evolution of our earth as she transforms.

Selected Resource List on Channeling

Books

Anka, Darryl   *The New Meta-physics*
Channeled through Bashar
Self-published
9940 Robbins, #204, Beverly Hills, CA 90212

Batholomew   *I Come As A Brother*
High Mesa Press, 1986

Carey, Ken   *The Starseed Transmissions*
Uni-Sun, 1982

Chandley, Dr. Margo   *A Psychological Investigation of The Development of The Mediumistic Process in Personality Function*
Self-published
9940 Robbins, #204, Beverly Hills, CA 90212

de Rohan, Ceanne   *The Right Use of Will*
Four Winds Publications, 1986

Klimo, Jonathan   *Channeling: Investigations on Receiving Information from Paranormal Sources*
Tarcher, 1987

Roberts, Jane *The Nature of Personal Reality*
Prentice-Hall, 1970; Bantam 1976
Psychic Politics: An Aspect Psychology Book
Prentice-Hall, 1976
The Seth Material
Prentice-Hall 1970; Bantam 1976

Roman, Sanaya *Living with Joy*
Kramer, 1986
Opening to Channel
Kramer, 1987
Personal Power Through Awareness
Kramer, 1986

Periodicals
Metapsychology: The Journal of Discarnate Intelligence
Editor: Tam Mossman
P.O. Box 3295, Charlottesville, VA 22903

Videocassettes
The Complete Guide to Channeling
Penny Price Productions
670 El Medio
Pacific Palisades, CA 90272

Audio Cassettes
Channeling by Kathryn Ridall, Ph.D.
Bantam Audio
666 Fifth Avenue
New York, NY 10103

Channeling by Kathryn Ridall, Ph.D.
is also available in Australia.
Contact: Transworld Publishers
           15-23 Helles Avenue
           Moorebank, N.S.W. 2170

LuminEssence Productions
Tapes by Sanaya Roman & Orin
P.O. Box 19117
Oakland, CA 94619

Additional Resources
Center For Applied Intuition
2046 Clement St.
San Francisco, CA
Director: Bill Kautz

Manifesting Inner Light Seminars
Instruction In Channeling Art
Judith Cornell, Ph.D.
15 Pearl St.
Sausalito, CA 94965

Seminars with Darryl Anka and Bashar
Interplanetary Connection
16161 Ventura Blvd. #314
Encino, CA 91436